M. M. D. L. T.

The History of Ayder Ali Khan, Nabob-Bahader

Or, new memoirs concerning the East Indies. With historical notes. Vol. 1

M. M. D. L. T.

The History of Ayder Ali Khan, Nabob-Bahader
Or, new memoirs concerning the East Indies. With historical notes. Vol. 1

ISBN/EAN: 9783337316501

Printed in Europe, USA, Canada, Australia, Japan

Cover: Foto ©ninafisch / pixelio.de

More available books at **www.hansebooks.com**

THE
HISTORY
OF
AYDER ALI KHAN,

NABOB-BAHADER:

OR,

New Memoirs concerning the *East Indies*.

WITH HISTORICAL NOTES.

By M. M. D. L. T.

General of Ten thousand Men in the Army of the Mogol
Empire, and formerly Commander in Chief of the
Artillery of Ayder Ali, and of a Body of European
Troops in the Service of that Nabob.

IN TWO VOLUMES.

VOL. I.

LONDON;

PRINTED FOR J. JOHNSON, N° 72,
ST. PAUL'S CHURCH-YARD.
M.DCC.LXXXIV.

ADVERTISEMENT.

THE proper names of places, perſons, and things, are for the moſt part given, in this Tranſlation, according to the orthography of the original; and a few expreſſions that relate to the ſtate of affairs at the time the Hiſtory was compoſed are ſtill retained, though ſubſequent events, particularly the death of Ayder, have rendered them leſs applicable at preſent.

AUTHOR'S PREFACE.

THOUGH it is not ufual to write the hiftory of a living prince, the great diftance which, in the prefent inftance, permits the hiftorian to fpeak with freedom, will ferve as an excufe for the infringement of fo juft a rule, in the eyes of thofe who may read the following fheets without prejudice. The writer has adhered to the ftricteft impartiality, in relating the exploits of the moft famous conqueror India has beheld fince the time of Thamas Kouli Khan ; a prince very much fuperior to that ufurper, as well for the extent of his genius as for the propriety of his conduct, which far exceeds that of the other Indian fovereigns.

It will be eafily perceived that the Author has neither endeavoured to flatter nor to calumniate. If the Englifh fhould find that they are not fpared, it will not be in their power to reproach him with having invented any untruth : and there are very many individuals of that nation, who know that he could fpeak much more effectually to the difadvantage of the Englifh

lifh adminiftration in India, if he thought it neceffary to reveal fuch particulars as he himfelf
has feen.

Whether the tyranny which thefe men have
exercifed in India be a crime of their nation, or
purely their own, is of no importance to the
Author in his capacity as an Hiftorian, fince
he has not made any reflections on the fubject
in the enfuing pages.

The Generals Coote, Smith, and Goddard,
are fpoken of with the juftice they deferve;
which circumftance ought to be of weight to
vindicate his impartiality from the reproaches
that interefted and prejudiced readers will doubtlefs be ready to make.

If any of his recitals fhould be contrary to
the ideas of certain perfons acquainted with the
fame events, he begs they will pleafe to make a
diftinction between the facts he himfelf has been
witnefs to, and thofe he could only learn from the
information of others.

The perfons cited in the courfe of the hiftory,
and who may be now in Europe, are appealed
to with confidence to affert the truth of what
is here attributed to them.   With regard to
other facts, it is requefted that they will believe
this narration in preference to what may have
been written to them by men who have not been

Z   in

in the fame confidential fituation as the Author, and have likewife reafons for difguifing the truth, that can have no influence upon him.

The true dignity and importance of hiftory is placed in truth. It has not therefore been in his power to fpare fuch of his countrymen as have behaved unworthily : but, out of confideration for their refpectable families, he has been careful to omit mentioning their names ; which is the only tendernefs he has indulged himfelf in. The following work is not ftrictly confined to the actions of Ayder Ali Khan ; but is likewife intended to give an accurate idea of the revolutions that have taken place in India, previous to the aggrandizement of that great prince : for the purpofe of fatisfying the reader on this head, it is thought proper to prefix an Hiftorical Introduction, that will render him acquainted with the genius and character of the perfonages fpoken of.

The account of particular circumftances relating to the Life of Ayder Ali Khan, that follows the Introduction, gives an idea of his perfon, confidered as a man, a general, and a foldier. The Author hopes that it will ferve to make the private character of the Nabob better known than thofe of moft European fovereigns. A perfect acquaintance with the men that furround

round a king, will often give the moſt accurate knowledge of his own manners and incli-
nations. With this intention, the portraits of
ſome of the relations as well as of the intimate
friends of Ayder are given.

There has not yet appeared any work that
explains the principles of government of the
princes now reigning in Indoſtan : it is therefore
hoped that the Public will receive with pleaſure the detail here given of the eſtabliſhments,
laws, cuſtoms, and forms of government that
prevail in Ayder's dominions. The Engliſh
have lately publiſhed the laws and cuſtoms of
the Hindoos : but Indoſtan has been ſo long governed by Mahometan princes, that this code
of the ancient Hindoo laws inſtruĉts us in the
preſent government of India, nearly as much as
the laws of the ancient Druids are capable of
explaining the adminiſtration and government of
the preſent French nation.

It is thought proper to give a map, on which
all the operations of Ayder may be followed. It
was not poſſible to do this on any of the charts
hitherto publiſhed, as there is not one among
them that gives a plan of Indoſtan ſufficiently
juſt to be of any ſervice to a traveller.

One of the greateſt difficulties that attend the
conſtruĉtion of maps of India, ariſes from the
different

different names that are given to provinces and towns, in the different languages fpoken in India. Three-fourths of the names given by the ancient inhabitants of the place, are not known even on the fpot. This arifes from the cuftom of the Moors or Mogols, who have changed the greater part of the names, and it is the Mogol names that are commonly ufed. In the map annexed to thefe Memoirs, the names moft in ufe are adopted; and the differences between this and other maps are founded on local knowledge and good obfervations.

The Author can with juftice indulge the hope that thefe Memoirs will not be confounded with thofe rhapfodies that have appeared within the laft three or four years, under the title of *Effais fur la Vie*, and *Abrégés de l'Hiftoire d'Hyder Ali*, which were evidently fabricated by people who have not only been totally unacquainted with Ayder, but even entirely without any memoirs, except thofe tales that have occafionally appeared in the public papers. From thefe materials, copied with fervility, they have formed compofitions which they have had the affurance to offer as original to the Public, under a variety of pompous titles. It was from a view of thefe inaccurate and fictitious compilations, that the Author was induced to write the Hiftory he now prefents to the world. As an eye-witnefs of part of his conquefts, and of the glory that furrounds him, he thought it a kind of duty incumbent on him to make this fovereign known, at an inftant in which he has become fo interefting to Europe, and to France in particular.

It will be perceived that the orthography of this work differs much from that of the public papers, which always write Hyder, inftead of Ayder, his true name. We have the authority of M. Buffi for this mode of fpelling, as may be feen by confulting the Memoirs of that gentleman, who refided many years at Ayder Abad, and could not be deceived in the name; any more than others who have been in Ayder's army, where the anfwer to *Qui vive?* or, *Who are you for?* is always, *Ayder Ali Khan, Nabob Bahader.* The true reafon of this is, that all our newswriters copy from the Englifh papers, who write *Hy,* which in their language is pronounced like the French *Ay.* The Englifh, in writing a foreign proper name, ufe fuch a combination of letters as gives the original found to an Englifh reader. And fince writing is the picture of fpeech, or the art of fpeaking to the eyes, why fhould not our tranflators follow their example?

THE

THE

HISTORY

OF

AYDER ALI KHAN.

INTRODUCTION.

BEFORE we enter upon the History of Ayder Ali Khan, it is neceſſary to give an account of part of thoſe revolutions, which the invaſion of India by Nadir Sha, king of Perſia, commonly called Thamas Kouli Khan, occaſioned in that extenſive empire; and more eſpecially in thoſe provinces that were the theatre of the various ſcenes we are about to relate.

Nadir Sha, previous to his quitting Delhi for the purpoſe of returning to his own ſtates,

concluded

concluded a treaty with Mehemet Sha, emperor of the Mogols, in which it was ordained that the charge of Grand Vifir, and all the Subafhips or viceroyalties *, then nine in number, fhould be hereditary in the families at that time in poffeffion of them. This article was doubtlefs a ftroke of politics in the Perfian conqueror, to divide the force of an empire, whofe ftrength was fufficiently exhibited in the army of 1,200,000 men affembled to oppofe him; and which, under an emperor of another difpofition, might revenge the infult fuftained by Mehemet Sha. But it is likewife to be prefumed, that he had previoufly fettled this point; and in putting it in execution, he only forwarded the ambitious views of Nizam El Moulouc, Grand Vifir and Suba of Decan, who, in revenge for an affront put upon him by Mehemet Sha, had invited the king of Perfia into the empire, and had been the means of

---

* The title, power, and prerogatives of a Suba cannot be better defined than by tranflating the word into the terms Vicar-general of the Empire. For this charge beftows a fupremacy over the kings and vaffals of the empire, which the Suba exercifes in the fame manner as the emperor himfelf. Similar to this would be the power of a vicar-general of the empire in Italy, if this dignity were at prefent poffeffed of activity and energy.

preferving

preferving him from the probable effects of fo rafh an undertaking.

The Subafhip of Decan, then in poffeffion of Nizam El Moulouc, conftituted at leaft a third part of the Mogol empire. All the country that extends from the gulf of Cambaya to Bengal, formed part of this Subafhip, whofe chief cities were Aurengabade and Ayderabade ; and it extended to all the coafts of the hither peninfula, from Cambaya to the gulf of Bengal.

This vaft government was divided into many others. Among thefe were many kingdoms governed by their own kings and particular laws, being no more than tributaries to the empire ; except that they were obliged to furnifh a certain number of troops to the army of the Suba, which the kings themfelves very often efteemed it an honour to lead in perfon. The principal of thefe kingdoms were thofe of the Marattas, of Canara, and of Mayffour.

Many of thefe kingdoms and ftates were fcarcely in fubjection ; and among them Canara, a country difficult of accefs from its numerous forefts and mountains. The Marattas were no otherwife fubjected, than by means of the treaty with the Suba, refpecting the payment of the Chotay, or fifth part of the revenue of De-

can,

can, which the emperor Aurengzebe had granted them ; and the great population of their
country furnifhed them with numerous and
powerful armies, efpecially of cavalry, whofe
incurfions were not eafily checked : And laftly
there were ftates, which, tho' comprized in
the Subafhip of Decan, were not yet fubjected.
Such were the fmall kingdom of Calicut, or of
the Samorins, and the other ftates of the black
princes on the coaft of Malabar ; into which
the armies of the Mogols were unable to pene-
trate, by reafon of the narrow and difficult en-
trances through forefts and mountains.

Befides the kingdoms and other tributary
countries, the Subafhip of Decan comprehended feveral governments, of greater or lefs magnitude, which were not hereditary, but in the
gift of the Suba ; whofe nomination, however,
required to be confirmed by the emperor.

When the Subafhips became hereditary, the
Subas pretended to the right of irrevocably no-
minating thofe governors, which the Europeans
call Nabobs, without the neceffity of any confirmation from the court of Dehli.

The Nabobfhip of Arcot * held the firft rank
among

* This Hiftory of the Nabobfhip of Arcot is very
different from that given by the Editor of the Memoirs
afcribed

among all thofe governments comprized in the Subafhip of Decan, as well for its extent as for its riches and population. For it contains all the country, known by the name of Coromandel, that lies between the mountains and the fea coaft, from Cape Comorin to Kifna, a river which, after running over a courfe of more than five hundred leagues, all within the Subafhip of Decan, falls into the fea near Mazulipatnam.

afcribed to general Lawrence. It is neceffary, in that work, to diftinguifh the reports of the Author himfelf from the account of the expeditions of general Lawrence. The latter is generally true, excepting that the French forces are magnified in number, and the Englifh diminifhed; fo as frequently to produce contradictions. As to the Editor of thofe Memoirs, it will be fufficient to form a judgment of him, if we recollect that he affirms, that, previous to the time in which M. Buffi followed Mouzaferzing, the Europeans were ignorant of what paffed at the court of the Indian princes, their neareft neighbours. He affirms likewife, in his introduction, that his work is defigned to exhibit or make known the rights of Mehemet Ali Khan. With this intention, he is careful to avoid every thing that can ferve to render him odious, as well as his father Anaverdi Khan. To fhew, from an inconteftable fact, that this Editor was not in poffeffion of accurate information, we need only obferve, that he gives Nizam El Moulouc no more than four fons, though he left fix. The two that are omitted by him are ftill living. The one is named Bazaletzing, and the other Mirs Mogol.

B 3 This

This government, though held only at the pleasure of the Suba, had been very long in possession of the same family, a branch of the Seyds, or descendants of Mahomet, by Ali his cousin and Fatima his daughter. The princes of this illustrious family were adored by their subjects, for having rendered the country rich and populous by the mildness and moderation of their government.

Several lords of the same family, as the Nabobs * of Veilour, Vandevachi, &c. possessed small tracts of country, which they had received *en appanage* †; but they acknowledged the Nabob of Arcot as their superior, and the chief of their family. This Nabobship of Arcot comprehended also several less states, as that of the Raja of Tanjaor, of the Naies of Madura, and of Mazara, &c. who were tributaries, and obliged to furnish a quota of troops to the Nabob's army.

In the year 1740, the Marattas made an incursion into the Subaship of Decan, in the absence of Nizam El Moulouc, Grand Visir

* The signification of the word Nabob will be hereafter explained.

† Lands are given *en appanage*, when they are in lieu of the future right of succession to the whole, of which they are a part.

and

and Suba; and, spreading like a torrent, they arrived at the country of Arcot, under the conduct of Ragogi their general.

The Nabob of Arcot * having collected his forces, which were by no means equal to those of the Marattas, marched against them, and lost both the victory and his life.

This unfortunate Nabob left an only son †, who succeeded him in his government. The rest of his family sought an asylum at Pondicherry, where the Sieur Dumas, then governor, received and promised to protect them, in return for the repeated advantages the French had received from the Nabobs of Arcot, since their first establishment in India.

Ragogi laid siege to Pondicherry, whose fortifications were in a very indifferent state. He demanded the governor to deliver up to him the family of the Nabob, and to pay him tribute. The spirited answer of the governor is well known. He replied, that *the dominions of the King of France had always been the asylum of unfortunate Princes; and that the French had no other tribute to give than bullets and*

---

* Daoust Ali Khan.
† Sabder Ali Khan.

B 4

balls.

balls. A piece of gallantry made to the miſ-
treſs of the Maratta general, contributed, together with the activity of the beſieged, to induce
Ragogi to raiſe the ſiege.

The ſame general, in the following year,
beſieged · Trichnapoli, a ſtrong place on the
river Caveri. It ſurrendered for want of pro-
viſion ; and Chanda Saeb, the Nabob of the
country, became priſoner, and was carried to
Sattara. Nizam El Moulouc, being informed
of the irruption of the Marattas and the death
of the Nabob of Arcot, who was aſſaſſinated,
nominated Anaverdi Khan, one of his beſt generals, a man of addreſs and of conſummate
knowledge in politics and the ſcience of government, regent and adminiſtrator of the government of Arcot, during the minority of the
young prince, Seyd Mehemet Khan, grandſon
of Daouſt Ali Khan. Anaverdi Khan, who then
(in 1742) commanded the forces of the Suba
of Decan to the northward of Maſulipatnam,
very ſoon arrived at Arcot. On the other
ſide, Nizam El Moulouc advancing by forced
marches to the relief of his dominions, Ragogi abandoned the country of Arcot, and retired into the country of the Marattas.

Anaverdi

Anaverdi Khan reſtored tranquillity and good order to the country entruſted to his charge, and made his government beloved both by the people and the army. He ſeemed at firſt to be exceedingly attached to the young prince, and was very attentive to the care of his education. But this inſidious politician, whoſe deſires tended ſolely to the acquiſition of his pupil's territories, was careful to inſpire the young prince with a degree of haughtineſs and avidity capable of rendering him odious, at the ſame time that he was himſelf courting every day more and more the affection of the people and the army.

When the young prince became of an age proper to marry, he adviſed him to eſpouſe the daughter of the Nabob of Veilour, one of his near relations. This Nabob having accepted the alliance with joy, propoſed to give ſuperb entertainments on the occaſion of the marriage, according to the ordinary cuſtom of the Indians, who are much attached to pomp and ceremony in circumſtances of this nature.

During the time of the preparation for the nuptials, at the beginning of the year 1744, Anaverdi Khan inſpired the young prince, who had the higheſt confidence in his tutor, with the

7   abſurd

abfurd idea of profiting by the tumult of the occafion, to get poffeffion of Veilour, and rob his
future father-in-law of the fortrefs, which
was the ftrongeft in all the country, and contained, as it was faid, a great mafs of treafure.   The young Nabob, whofe heart was
already corrupted, approved highly of this advice, and refolved to put it in execution.   He
repaired to Veilour, where it was concerted
that Anaverdi Khan fhould caufe foldiers to
come as fimple fpectators, who, joining at once
with the prince's retinue and thofe who accompanied Anaverdi Khan, fhould put the garrifon
of Veilour to the fword, and take poffeffion of
the place, according to the orders of the young
prince.   But the perfidious tutor, who had de-
vifed this confpiracy with no other intention
than that of betraying his pupil into deftruction, fent but a fmall number of foldiers; and
caufed the Nabob of Veilour to be advifed fecretly of the defign of his nephew, the evening
before he had appointed to come himfelf to the
place.   His hope was, that the Nabob, enraged at the perfidy of his future fon-in-law,
would put him to death.   In this, however,
he was difappointed; for the Nabob contented
himfelf with reproaching the young man publicly

licly with his crime; and caufed him to leave the place immediately, with all his followers.

The event of this contrivance having turned out contrary to the expectations of Anaverdi Khan, he foon after formed another plot, which fucceeded in accomplifhing the deftruction of the young Nabob.

Nizam El Moulouc being defirous of poffeffing an army, which, though compofed of different Indian nations become effeminate by a long peace, fhould neverthelefs be fit for the purpofes of war, had with that intention invited into his dominions a great number of Patanes, or inhabitants of Candahar, the remains of thofe Agwans who had conquered Perfia, and whom Nadir Sha, after having chaced them out of that fertile kingdom, had purfued even to their own mountains. He had even beftowed among the chiefs of them Nabobfhips, or fiefs of the empire; whence arofe the Patane Nabobs of Carpet, Canour, and Sanour,— a numerous corps of thefe Patanes, who compofed part of the Nabob of Arcot's army, and to whom, at that time, confiderable fums were due for pay. Thefe people are courageous; but ferocious, cruel, and perfidious,

fidious, when they believe themfelves ill-treated. Anaverdi Khan affembled thefe Patanes at Arcot, under the pretence of caufing them to pafs in review before their prince; and, by his fecret agents, excited them to demand the arrears of pay due to them. He did not fail to advife the young Nabob, that the method to enforce refpect from his troops, was to threaten them with the chaftifement due to their infolence. The prince, who was but too much inclined to fpeak with haughtinefs and contempt, treated them in the fevereft manner. A revolt was the confequence; and, in their fury, they did not fpare even the Nabob himfelf, but put him to the fword. This event happened early in the year 1745.

Anaverdi Khan, arrived at the height of his defires, affected to be oppreffed with the utmoft defpair and forrow. He continued for fome time to deplore the lofs of his pupil; but at length becoming gradually more moderate, and the Patanes appearing to be concerned for the effects of their ferocity, he perfuaded them that he would refer the affair to the decifion of Nizam. But in the mean time he fecretly affembled the chiefs of all the other corps of the army, and reprefented to them, that, fince

the

the Grand Vifir would confound them all with the criminals, there was but one way of juftifying themfelves, namely, to extirpate the Patanes. The infolent ferocity of thofe foldiers had rendered them odious to all the other Indians; and the advice of Anaverdi Khan was therefore univerfally approved of. The effect of their deliberation was kept a profound fecret; and they feized an opportunity fo favourable to their purpofe, that all the Patanes, to the number of 3000, were maffacred, the women and children only being fpared *.

Anaverdi Khan, having at length finifhed this horrible carnage, wrote to Nizam El Moulouc the hiftory of the cataftrophe of the young

* As thefe anecdotes are differently related elfewhere, it may happen that many, who think themfelves intimately acquainted with the hiftory of India, may demand, How the Writer of thefe Memoirs could acquire his knowledge of them? To anticipate this queftion, it is anfwered, that they cannot but know that the court and army of Ayder are filled with the relations and fervants of the ancient family of the Nabobs of Arcot. Such are Razafaeb, the Nabob of Vandevachi, the fon-in-law and nephew of the Nabob of Veilour; Affinfaeb, an old man of great merit, formerly grand-treafurer of the Nabobs of Arcot, and exercifing

young Nabob of Arcot, and the punifhment he had caufed to be inflicted on the Patanes; arranging the whole account to his own advantage. The Grand Vifir, Suba of Decan, concluded that he could not do better than to beftow the Nabobfhip on Anaverdi Khan; as the family of the ancient Nabobs was extinct, and Chanda Saeb, who by right of his wife might pretend to it, was prifoner among the Marattas.

At the end of the year 1745, Anaverdi Khan was eftablifhed Nabob of Arcot, but did not fuccced in procuring the fame refpect for his government as had attended his regency. He had feveral children. Maffous Khan, his cldeft fon, was defigned for his fucceffor; but his predilection was in favour of a fon whom the

---

exercifing the fame office under Ayder Ali Khan. In the fame army are likewife Baoud Khan and Savay Khan, brothers, and chiefs of the Patanes, ftrongly attached to the French; and, by reafon of their youth, fpared in the maffacre caufed by Anaverdi Khan. The Author of this work being defirous of informing himfelf in the hiftory of India, cultivated the friendfhip of all thefe perfons; who took a pleafure in relating the hiftory of the misfortunes of their family, their nation, and their ancient mafters. It is from them that he has learned the facts he relates in this place.

Iaw

law excluded from the fucceffion, as being born out of the houfe, and by a Bayadere, or woman reputed common.—He gave Trichnapoli, a ftrong place on the Caveri, with a confiderable territory, to this fon, who was named Mehemet Ali Khan.

Anaverdi Khan was in quiet poffeffion of the fruit of his crimes, when Providence raifed up an avenger of the family of the Nabobs of Arcot. This man was the famous Dupleix, whom the French King and Eaft India Company, in 1746, called from the employment of director and commandant of Chandenagor, and appointed governor of Pondicherry.

This great man, after having acquired much glory by his brave defence of Pondicherry againft Admiral Bofcawen, whom he forced to raife the fiege, received the news of the peace between France and England in the year 1747. In this juncture he thought it neceffary, for the honour and advantage of his nation, to punifh Anaverdi Khan for the affiftance he had afforded the Englifh during the fiege, by furnifhing them with troops on that occafion : being likewife well affured, that this new family would always oppofe the in-

terefts

terefts of the French, who had fhewn fo ftrong an attachment to the family of Seyd. His firft ftep was to procure an antagonift to Anaverdi Khan, by his negociations with the Marattas; who were by that means induced to fet at liberty Chanda Saeb, Nabob of Trichnapoli, who had efpoufed the fifter of the laft Nabob of Arcot, and whofe wife and fon had taken refuge at Pondicherry.

Chanda Saeb being thus reftored to his liberty, repaired immediately to the court cf Nazerzing, who fucceeded his father Nizam El Moulouc in the Subafhip of Decan in 1748. It was in vain that he folicited this young prince to re-eftablifh him in the Nabobfhip of Arcot, as the inheritance of his wife, or at leaft in his town and fortrefs of Trichnapoli: the intrigues and the money of Anaverdi Khan prevented his fuccefs with the Suba. But he was more fortunate in his application to Idadmoudi Khan, king of the little ftate of Adonis, and nephew of Nazerzing. This young prince, the fon of an elder brother of the Suba, had been defigned by Nizam El Moulouc as his fucceffor; but that Vifir perceiving himfelf at the point of death, and his grandfon very young,

young, nominated and caufed his fon Nazerzing to be acknowledged his fucceffor.

Chanda Saeb perfuaded the young prince of Adonis, that it was proper for him to requeft the Nabobfhip of Arcot of his uncle; the extent and value of this laft being much more confiderable than the territory of Adonis. The nephew confequently made his requeft, which met with a refufal from his uncle, whofe jealoufy made him averfe to a ftep that tended to increafe the power of his nephew. Idadmoudi Khan, urged on by Chanda Saeb and M. Dupleix, raifed an army of 60,000 men, with which, accompanied by Chanda Saeb, he arrived in the country of Arcot in July 1749, where he was joined by the French, to the number of 600 men and 2,000 Seapoys, commanded by the Comte D'Auteuil. This army marched againft Anaverdi Khan, who had affembled all his force, and encamped near Ambour. After having repulfed his antagonifts for two fuccefsfive days, his entrenchments were forced by the French on the third; and he loft the victory and his life at the age of eighty-two years. His two fons, Maffous Khan and Mehemet Ali Khan, were prefent at this battle. The firft was made prifoner, and the other fled to the fortrefs of Trichnapoli. Every other part of the country acknowledged the grandfon of Nizam El Moulouc, as Nabob of Arcot.

Nazerzing, jealous of the acceffion of power that Idadmoudi Khan had acquired, contrary to his orders affembled his army, and marched into the country of Arcot againft him, Chanda Saeb, and the French who had affifted him in his undertaking. And in the month of February 1750, he arrived within fix leagues of Pondicherry, with an innumerable army.

The ancient minifters and courtiers of Nizam El Moulouc, fhocked to behold this diffention, attempted to reconcile the uncle and the nephew. They concerted among themfelves, that the nephew fhould repair to his uncle's camp, and make his fubmiffion; and that the uncle fhould inveft him with the authority of Nabob of Arcot. Idadmoudi Khan, on the affurances of the lords who had offered themfelves as mediators, repaired to the camp of Nazerzing; who, inftead of giving him the appointment of Nabob, caufed him to be arrefted.

This treachery of the Suba of Decan occafioned a general difguft in his whole army. The lords confpired his deftruction, and correfponded

with

with the governor Dupleix, who caufed the French army, confifting of 800 French and 4,000 Seapoys, under M. de la Touche, to march againft the army of Nazerzing, confifting of more than 300,000 fighting men. But this handful of French, aided by the confpirators, were fufficient to decide the fate of fo powerful a prince, who was flain on his elephant by the Patane Nabob of Carpet, one of the confpirators. His nephew Idadmoudi Khan fucceeded to his government, as Suba, in the month of December, in the fame year.

It is at this æra that the hiftory of Ayder Ali Khan commences in thefe Memoirs. He was then at the head of a fmall quota of troops in Nazerzing's army, being about twenty-two years old. It would be difficult to trace his actions from a more remote period; becaufe, being born a private individual, no perfon has taken the pains to collect the facts that relate to his infancy. They were far from beholding the avenger of India, in the foldier of Nazerzing; or the fcourge of the Englifh, in the army that then fought againft the French.

Idadmoudi Khan, who affumed the name of Mouza Ferzing, expreffed his gratitude to M. Dupleix and all the French, and gave the Na-

bobfhip

bobſhip of Arcot to Chanda Saeb. In his return to Ayder Abad, his capital, he was accompanied by M. de Buſſi, at the head of a
body of French troops ; but he was not fortunate enough to arrive at the end of his voyage,
the Patanes having ſlain him in a ſedition.
At the beginning of 1751, his uncle Salaberzing, brother of Nazerzing, ſucceeded him,
and had the ſame affection for the French as
his nephew. Mr. Lally having recalled M.
Buſſi, in 1758, from the court and army of
Salaberzing, this prince, whoſe diſpoſition was
good, though his abilities were not great, was
aſſaſſinated by his brother Nizam Ali Khan,
who is at preſent Suba of Decan, and will
frequently be mentioned in the courſe of the
following Hiſtory.

The Engliſh having always ſupported the
family of Anaverdi Khan, preferred Mehemet
Ali Khan to his eldeſt brother ; and cauſed him
to be acknowledged Nabob of Arcot in the
treaty of Fontainebleau, after having aſſiſted
him to impoveriſh all the princes of the ancient family of the Nabobs of Arcot. Chanda
Saeb had the misfortune to fall into the hands
of the Engliſh, who were cruel enough to deliver him to Menagi, general of the troops at

Tanjaor,

Tanjaor, who caufed him to be beheaded in the month of June 1752. This crime, though yet unrevenged, will not pafs unpunifhed ; for Ayder Ali has promifed the dominions of the Raja of Tanjaor to Raza Saeb, fon of Chanda Saeb.

This fuccinct account of the revolutions in India, is fufficient to ferve as an introduction to the Hiftory of Ayder Ali Khan.

Note.—The Cofs is an Indian meafure of diftance, which anfwers nearly to 2500 toifes, or a few yards more than an Englifh league.

PARTICULAR CIRCUMSTANCES

RELATING TO THE

PERSON, HABITS, AND MANNERS

O F

AYDER ALI KHAN.

AYDER Ali Khan, whofe precife age is not known, ought to be about fifty-four or fifty-fix years of age, if we may depend on thofe who have known him from his infancy. He is about five feet fix inches high, and very lufty, though active, and capable of bearing fatigue as well on foot as on horfe-back. His complexion is very brown, as is that of all Indians who expofe themfelves to the air and the fun. His features are coarfe, his nofe fmall and turned up, his lower lip rather thick; and he wears neither beard nor whif-kers, contrary to the cuftom of the Orientals, efpecially the Mahometans. His habits, like thofe of all the natives of India, are of white

muflin,

muflin, with a turban of the fame. His robe
is fafhioned nearly the fame as thofe of the
European ladies, which are called *à l'Angloife*.
The body and fleeves fit neatly, and are drawn
clofe by ftrings ; the reft of the robe being
ample, and in folds : fo that when the Indian
great men walk, a page fupports their train,
from their firft ftepping off the carpet to their
entering into their carriages.

In the army, Ayder Ali wears a military habit invented by himfelf for his generals. It is an
uniform compofed of a veft of white fattin, with
gold flowers, faced with yellow, and attached by
cords or ftrings of the fame colour : the drawers
are of the fame materials ; and the boots of yellow velvet. He wears a fcarf of white filk
about his waift ; and, with the military habit,
his turban is of a red or aurora colour. When
he is on foot, he commonly ufes a gold-headed
cane ; and fometimes on horfeback he wears
a fabre, hanging by a belt of velvet embroidered with gold, and faftened over his fhoul-
der by a clafp of gold, enriched with fome precious ftones.

He never wears jewelry either on his turban or his clothes ; and never ufes either neck-
lace, ear-pendants, or bracelets. His turban
is

is very long, and flat at top. In this particular he follows the ancient mode; as well as
in his flippers, which are very large, and have
a long point turned back, refembling the roofs
of the buildings in fome countries up the Le-
vant; or thofe flippers anciently worn in
France, and called *Souliers à la poulaine.* The
petits maîtres of his and other Indian courts
affect to wear little bonnets which fcarcely cover the tops of their heads, and flippers fo
fmall as fcarce to admit the points of their
feet: but though in thefe and other refpects
their tafte is fo different from that of Ayder
and his fon, yet to imitate him as much as
poffible in the article of beard and whifkers,
without infringing the precepts of the Alcoran, they reduce their beard and mouftaches to
a mouftache fcarcely difcernible.

The countenance of Ayder, though not
handfome, is open, and calculated to infpire
confidence. He has not acquired the habit of
difguifing his afpect, which is either gay or
overfpread with chagrin, according to the oc-
cafions that prefent themfelves. He poffeffes
a facility of converfing on any fubject; and
has none of that ftatelinefs and taciturnity,
which almoft all the other princes of the Eaft
affect

affect to preferve. When he receives a ftranger, he is referved, and appears to fpeak with gravity; but foon recovers his ufual eafe, and converfes with all the world, repeating himfelf the news and common converfation of the day, with the greateft affability. It is moft aftonifhing, that this fovereign afks queftions, gives anfwers, hears a letter read, and dictates an anfwer to another, beholds a theatrical exhibition, and even feems to attend to the performance,—at the fame inftant that he decides concerning things of the utmoft importance.

There is no fovereign more eafy of accefs to every one that has bufinefs with him, whether ftrangers or fubjects; and the former, whatever may be their quality, are always fure to be introduced into his prefence, by demanding an audience, by a Souquedar, or macebearer, of which there is always a fufficient number at the gate of his palace. The Fakirs, a fpecies of begging monks, are alone excluded from this indulgence; but when one of thefe appears, he is conducted to the Pirjada, or grand almoner, who fupplies his wants. The court of Ayder is, in this point, abfolutely different from thofe of all the other

princes of India ; who hold thefe Fakirs in
fuch high veneration, that they fuffer them to
enter their palaces at any hour, and even admit them to their table. They have the affurance to take the firft place at table, neareft
the prince ; though they are moft commonly
difgufting, filthy, and covered with vermin.

When bufinefs or parties of pleafure do not
prevent Ayder Ali from going to reft at his
ufual time, which is after midnight, he rifes
with the fun, that is to fay, about fix o'clock.
As foon as he is rifen, the majors of the army *,
who have been on duty the preceding day and
night, and likewife thofe who relieve them,
enter, make their reports, and receive orders to
be tranfmitted to the minifters and generals,
who themfelves have the privilege of entering
his dreffing-room, if they have any thing extraordinary or preffing to communicate. The
couriers that have arrived during the night, or
in the morning, alfo come and lay their difpatches at his feet. It may be efteemed a
weaknefs in a prince fo occupied, that his toi-

* Thefe majors of the army are like adjutants-gene-
ral. They are not perfons of diftinction, but men of
approved diligence and fidelity, chofen out of the fub-
altern officers of cavalry and infantry.

let.

let takes up a confiderable part of his time. It lafts commonly two or three hours ; and is chiefly taken up by his barbers, who pluck the hairs from his beard.

' But juftice requires us likewife to obferve, that when any military operation requires his attention, the toilet is no more thought of.

Between eight and nine in the morning he quits his apartment, and repairs to a faloon, where a number of fecretaries wait for his ap-pearance. Into their hands, according to their refpective departments, he puts the letters received ; giving them at the fame time inftructions for the anfwers. His fons, his relations, and thofe lords who are honoured with his intimacy, enter ; and if it be nine o'clock, they take the ufual refrefhment. If he has leifure, he appears at a balcony, and receives the falute of his elephants *, that are led before him, as well as his horfes. His tygers of chace likewife pay him a vifit. They are led by hand, and are covered with a mantle of green and gold hanging to the ground, and

* When the prince appears at the balcony, his officers cry out, " Your elephants falute your Majefty :" And at the fame time thofe animals, who are ranged in a femicircle round the palace, make three genuflections.

a bonnet

a bonnet on their head, of cloth embroidered
with gold, with which their eyes can be immediately covered, if they fhould chance to prove
mifchievous. Ayder himfelf gives each of them
a ball of fweetmeats, which they take very
adroitly with their paws, being exceedingly
tame. Thefe are the fpotted tygers, and their
keepers lead them every day into thofe places
where the greateft crowds are : but the grand
tyger, or tyger royal, has never been tamed by
any attempts yet made.

After the repaft, which ends about half after
ten, Ayder enters into the hall of audience ;
or the grand tent, if at the army. He is
feated on a fopha beneath a canopy, and very
often in fome balcony that fronts an open
place or court of the palace ; and fome of his
relations fit on each fide of him. All perfons
who have permiffion or accefs, of which the
number is very great, may come to this audience ; and thofe who have affairs to tranfact,
may either requeft admittance by means of the
Souquedars, or put their requeft into the hands
of thofe officers by whom it is carried to their
chief, who is always prefent, and who places
it at the feet of the prince, where it is immediately read and anfwered. It is not cuftomary

here

here to ſtop the prince by the offer of peti-
tions, when he goes out, unleſs the affair be
very urgent and extraordinary, or the peti-
tioner has been prevented from forwarding his
requeſt at the uſual hours of audience : a cir-
cumſtance that very rarely happens *.

At

* In the year 1767, Ayder being at Coilmoutour,
and going out with his retinue, about five in the evening, to take the air, an old woman proſtrated herſelf,
and cried out, Juſtice!—Ayder immediately cauſed
his carriage to ſtop; made a ſign to her to come forward, and demanded her requeſt. She anſwered, My
Lord, I had but one daughter, and Aggi Mahmout
has raviſhed her from me. Ayder replied, Aggi
Mahmout has been gone hence more than a month;
how does it happen that you have waited till this
time without complaining?—My Lord, I have given
many requeſts into the hands of Ayder Sha, and have
received no anſwer.—This Ayder Sha, who was the
chief uſher, preceded the Nabob, bearing a large collar of gold, as a mark of his dignity. He advanced,
and ſaid, This woman, as well as her daughter, are
of infamous repute, and live in a diſgraceful manner. The Nabob gave orders to return inſtantly to
the palace, and commanded the woman to follow him.
All the court were in great apprehenſion for the officer,
who was much beloved; and no perſon daring to intercede for him, the ſon of Ayder begged the commandant of Europeans to endeavour to procure his
pardon. He accordingly requeſted it of Ayder, who
refuſed it with much ſeverity. I cannot grant your
requeſt,

At this audience thirty or forty ſecretaries
are ſeated along the wall to his left, who write
continually: Couriers arrive almoſt every inſtant, and are conducted with great noiſe and

requeſt, ſaid he: there is no greater crime than that
of interrupting the communication between a ſovereign and his ſubjects.   It is the duty of the powerful to ſee that the weak have juſtice.   The ſovereign
is the only protector God has given them; and the
prince who ſuffers oppreſſion to paſs unpuniſhed among
his ſubjects, is deſervedly deprived of their affection
and confidence, and at laſt compels them to revolt
againſt him.   He then gave orders to puniſh Ayder
Sha with two hundred ſtripes on the parade; and at
the ſame time commanded an officer of his Abyſſinian
horſe-guard to repair immediately with the woman to
the country ſeat at which Aggi Mahmout then was.
If he found the girl, his orders were, to deliver her
to her mother, and return with the head of Aggi
Mahmout; but if ſhe was not found, he was charged
to conduct Aggi Mahmout to Coilmoutour.   The girl
was found, and the head of the criminal was brought
to Ayder.   Aggi Mahmout was then ſixty years
old, had been chief uſher to Ayder Ali twenty-five
years, and was ſucceeded in his office by Ayder Sha;
at which time the Nabob had given him a Zoghir, or
conſiderable diſtrict of land, as a reward for his ſervices.   This man was enamoured of the girl, and had
carried her off, upon her mother's refuſing to ſell her
to him, becauſe ſhe ſubſiſted by proſtituting her.—The
Alcoran condemns the raviſher of a girl or woman to
death.

7.   buſtle

buftle to the feet of the prince, where they lay their difpatches. A fecretary kneeling takes the packet; and fitting on his hams before the prince, opens it and reads the letter. Ayder immediately dictates the particulars of the anfwer, and the letter is carried to the office of a minifter; contrary to the cuftoms of the princes of the Eaft, who affix their names by means of a feal. Ayder figns the difpatches in order as they are completed, as well as a number of private orders. Many writers report the contrary to this; which only proves that they have never feen Ayder half an hour at a time. The orders that iffue from the offices of the minifters, have no other fignature than that of the great feal, of which they are the depofitories; and the difpatch is clofed with the private feal of the minifter. The letters figned by Ayder are clofed by the feal of the fovereign, of which the principal fecretary is guardian. When this Nabob writes any interefting letter, or gives an order of importance, he affixes a particular or private feal, which he always wears on his finger; and in that cafe he himfelf carries the packet to one of his couriers, who conveys it as far as the firft ftation. To the packet is joined a paper, denoting the hour it was fent

off;

off; and at every ſtation the time of its arrival is marked. We ſhall afterwards have occaſion to ſpeak of theſe poſts, which have been ſince imitated by the Engliſh.

If Ayder purchaſes horſes or elephants, or if new pieces of cannon have been founded or brought from any port or arſenal, he inſpects them during this audience; the animals or pieces of cannon being brought into the court or ſquare of the palace.

Miniſters, generals, ambaſſadors, and other great men, rarely appear at this audience, unleſs commanded, or unleſs urged by extraordinary affairs. It is peculiar to their dignity to ſee the prince only in the evening, when none but men of conſequence are admitted; and nothing elſe is thought of but to make their court to the ſovereign, or to ſhare his pleaſures. The great have agents, who are uſually Bramins, who ſolicit their affairs either with the prince or his miniſters; and theſe agents, who have the title of Ouaquils, or envoys, have their leave of admiſſion to the preſence when they have been preſented by their maſters, and are honourably received. The miniſters ſend one of the principal ſecretaries of their department to the prince; who, ſitting before him in the

ſame

same posture as the other secretaries, communicate their business, and converse with him.

A great ambassador, or other person of consequence, is announced in a loud voice by the chief of the ushers, in these terms, " Your " Majesty, the Lord of —— salutes you." Ministers, secretaries, ouaquils, or other men of business, are not announced, but go in and out without particular observation, except that they are careful to salute the Nabob. When a great man is announced, the prince returns the salute, and begs him to be seated : the friends and other great men, who surround the sovereign, salute him also ; and, in proportion to the esteem or favour he is in with the Nabob, they give place, that he may approach him. A person of ordinary rank, who has requested an audience, makes three reverences in entering, by moving his hand from his forehead almost to the ground ; and afterwards places himself on one side of the chief usher, continuing silent, with his hands joined before him. The Nabob returns the salute by simply touching his turban with his hand, and affects to continue the discourse with those about him : after which he makes a sign for the person to advance, and demands, in an engaging and af-

fectionate

fectionate manner, the subject of his visit : and
upon the exposition of the affair by the sup-
pliant, he receives a decisive answer. If he be
a stranger of a genteel rank or employment,
as a trader or merchant of consequence, he
receives orders to sit ; and his place is usually
on the right, fronting the secretaries. The
Nabob asks him some questions respecting his
state of life, his country, or his voyage, and
appoints a time when he will see his merchan-
dizes. Betel is then presented to the stranger,
and is understood as equivalent to a permission
to retire ; which is done with the same ceremony as at the entrance.

This audience continues till after three o'clock,
which is the hour he returns to his apartment to
sleep, or make the siesto, as it is called in Italy.

About half past five, the prince returns into
the hall of audience, or some other large apartment, where he places himself in a balcony to
see his troops exercise, and his cavalry defile
before him. He is, as in the morning, sur-
rounded by some of his friends or relations ;
and the secretaries are busied in reading letters,
or writing.

About half after six, when the day closes in,
a great number of Manelsalgis, or bearers of

flambeaux,

flambeaux, appear in the court of the palace, and falute the prince as they pafs on the fide of the apartment where he is. They illuminate all the apartments in a moment, efpecially that in which the Nabob is, with tapers in chandeliers of exquifite workmanfhip, ornamented with feftoons of flowers of the utmoft lightnefs and delicacy. Thefe chandeliers, on account of the wind, are covered with large fhades of Englifh glafs. There are likewife, in fome parts of the palace, large glafs lanthorns, painted with flowers of all colours. The great men, minifters, and ambaffadors, vifit the Nabob only at night. They are ufually perfumed with the moft coftly perfumes. Befides the men in power and employment, the apartments are filled with young nobility; and every body affumes the moft polite and engaging manners. After having faluted the prince, the falute is paid to his fons and relations, his minifters, and others, in an eafy, unaffected manner. Among the young nobility, there are a certain number who have the title of Arabfbequi; which anfwers nearly to that of chamberlain, in Germany. There are ordinarily four in waiting each day: they are diftinguifhed by their fabre, which

D 2

they

they carry in their hand in the sheath, using it nearly as a walking-stick. All the other company leave their arms in the hands of their pages and other attendants, who are very numerous, and fill the avenues of the palace. The pages alone are permitted to enter: they follow their master, bearing his train into the apartments, till they quit their slippers at their stepping on the carpet: the pages then let fall the train, and put the slippers in a bag. Ayder, who sets no great value on these ceremonies, permits the Europeans to come in with their shoes on; though his apartments are commonly covered with white muslin, spread upon the most superb Persia carpets. He has such a predilection for white, that he causes wainscotting, that is painted, gilt, and varnished, to be covered with white muslin; and even chairs and sophas of embroidered velvet or gold stuff. The Europeans deceive themselves exceedingly in supposing, that it is by way of distinction or pre-eminence that they are permitted to enter the apartments in shoes. This permission, given them in some of the Indian courts, is occasioned by a notion the Indian princes have, that the Europeans are obstinate, and bigotted to their own customs,

I   however

however repugnant to decency and propriety.
M. de Buffi, to conciliate the Indian cuftoms
with thofe of the French, carried velvet flippers
to the court of the Suba of Decan, which he
put on; and made ufc of a kind of pantoufle in
paffing from his carriage to the border of the
carpet, where he threw them off. We may
often avoid offending ftrangers by little atten-
tions that coft nothing, and tend exceedingly
to conciliate their affections.

There is, for the moft part, a comedy every
night, that commences about eight in the
evening, and lafts till eleven : it is intermix-
ed with dances and fongs. During this comedy, the Arabfbequi continue near the ftrangers, and politely inform them of every thing
they may defire to know; as the fubject of
the comedy, the news of the day, &c. They
are careful to afk, if he chufes to drink or
eat; in which cafe, they caufe fherbet, warm
milk, fruits, or confectionary to be prefented to him ; but they feldom eat. If the
ftranger chufes to play chefs, they play with
him, or propofe a party. Ayder, to whom
the entertainments of the ftage are very indifferent, difcourfes with his minifters or ambaffadors, fometimes paffing into a cabinet

to fpeak with more fecrecy; and continues, as
in the morning, to difpatch bufinefs, without
feeming to be bufy. Almoft always, before
the end of the performance, flowers are brought
to him in a bafket of filigram, out of which
he himfelf gives a few to the lords who
are about him; and afterwards the bafket
is carried into the apartments of the theatre,
every one taking a fmall flower from them,
and returning a profound reverence to the
prince. This takes place even to the loweft
fecretary. When Ayder wifhes to give a particular mark of his efteem, he himfelf makes a
collar of jafmine flowers, knotting them with
filk as he converfes, which he himfelf adjufts
round the neck of the happy mortal to whom
he gives this glorious mark of his efteem and
favour. He has feveral times conferred this
honour on the chiefs of his Europeans, knowing well that the French, above all nations,
efteem themfelves well paid by this fort of
money. He who has received this honour, is
vifited the following day by the firft people of
the court to compliment him.

If a battle has been gained, or any other
glorious event has happened in favour of the
prince, the poet of the court arrives, announc-
ing

ing himfelf, at his firft entering the apartments, by the pompous and extravagant titles he be-ftows on the prince: as, " Health to the " greateft king on earth, whofe name alone " caufes his enemies to tremble," &c. All the world, at the voice of the poet, becomes filent and attentive. The comedy or dance is in-terrupted ; the poet enters, feats himfelf in the place immediately oppofite the prince, and re-cites a poem, which every body affects to hear with the utmoft attention, except the prince, who feems at that time to be more particularly bufied in converfing with his mi-nifters. The poet ufually, after fpeaking of the prince, proceeds to his relations, and the generals or principal officers ; not forgetting the minifters and favourites. The young courtiers, or *baras à demi*, who are ufually included altogether in the praifes beftowed by the poet, often turn it into ridicule ; and their derifion extends even to thofe who are the higheft fpoken of. They and the fecretaries, or other inferior courtiers, often parody the words of the poem very pleafantly, fparing no body but the prince and his fon : but as they have no printing, both the poem and the cri-ticifm are of fhort duration. We cannot

D 4

fpeak

fpeak of their public entertainments, without mentioning the Bayaderes, of whom the Abbé Raynal has drawn fo advantageous a portrait in his Hiftoire Philofophique.

At the prefent time, the court of Ayder is the moft brilliant in India ; and his company of performers is without contradiction the firft, as well on account of its riches, as becaufe the Bayaderes are the women to whom he gives the preference. Being fovereign of part of Vifapour, he has every facility of procuring, among this clafs of women, thofe who are moft remarkable for their beauty and talents.

·The comedians of the court are all women. A directrefs, who is likewife manager, purchafes young girls at the age of four or five years, who are chofen on account of their beauty. She caufes them to be inoculated, and then provides them with mafters both for dancing and mufic. · They are taught every accomplifhment that can infpire the prince and his court with the love of pleafure ; and their fuccefs is fuch, that they delight and feduce the moft infenfible of men. They begin to appear in public at the age of about ten or eleven years. They have generally the moft delicate features, large dark eyes, beautiful eye-brows,

fmall

fmall mouth, and the fineft teeth ; their cheeks are dimpled, and their black hair hangs in flowing trefles to the ground ; their complexion is a clear brown, not fuch as that of the Mulatto women, who are incapable of blufhing ; but like that of a country girl in the flow of health, who has preferved the rofes, after fuffering the lillies to fade. Thefe are the yellow women, that the Orientals prefer to all others : they give themfelves that tinge by painting their cheeks of a jonquil colour, in the fame manner as the French women ufe rouge ; and it is remarkable that in a very fhort time one becomes habituated to this colour, and finds it agreeable. Their habit is always a fine gauze, very richly embroidered with gold ; and they are covered with jewels : their head, their neck, their ears, their breafts, their arms, fingers, legs, and toes, have their jewels ; and even their nofe is ornamented with a fmall diamond, that gives them an arch look, which is far from being unpleafing.

The comedies are all pieces of intrigue. They perfonate either women who league together to deceive a jealous hufband, or young girls that confpire to deceive their mother. It is impoffible to play with more art or with more natural cafe.

eafe. Their fongs are gay and agreeable. The words that are fung by a fingle voice are almoft always the complaint of a lover. Thofe which are fung in chorus are much gayer ; but they have no fecond parts, and are always repeated.

The dancers are fuperior in their perform- ance to the comedians and fingers : it may even be affirmed that they would afford plea- fure on the theatre of the opera at Paris. Every part is employed when thefe girls dance ; their heads, their eyes, their arms, their feet, and all their body feem to move only to en- chant and furprife. They are very light, and very ftrong in the legs ; turning round on one foot, and fpringing up immediately after with a furprifing force. They have fo much accu- racy in their movements, that they accom- pany the inftruments with bells that are on their feet ; and as they are of the moft elegant figures, all their motions are graceful. No Bayadere of the prince's company is more than feventeen years old. At this age they are dif- miffed ; and either travel over the province, or attach themfelves to the Pagods *.

* Every Pagod maintains a number of Bayaderes, whofe charms produce one of the moft certain revenues of the Bramins.

The

The directrefs of this company is paid by the prince; but her emoluments are not known. She has always a number of pieces ready in rehearfal to be played at a moment's notice. Tho' there is every reafon to think fhe is well paid by Ayder for the pleafures fhe procures him, the emoluments fhe receives from private individuals of fortune, are ftill more advantageous to her. When a great man gives a fet fupper, he has ufually a comedy ornamented with fongs and dances. The directrefs of the prince's company is paid one hundred rupees for every actrefs that plays, fings, or dances. The number of thefe actreffes is often more than twenty, the inftrumental mufic not being charged.

If a fupper is given to a few private friends, the fingers and dancers are likewife employed at the fame price of one hundred rupees. Befides which, they muft be furnifhed with fupper, and abundance of fruits, fweetmeats, and warm milk. If the friends are retained to fleep (as is often done, where their fuppers are more friendly than ceremonious) they chufe each a companion for the night among the performers, for which the directrefs is likewife paid one hundred rupees each; and the mafter
of

of the houfe muft prefent his friend with fome trinket, or piece of ftuff, to be given to the damfel when fhe is fent away in the morning.

Befides the prince's company, there are feveral others in the town where the court is kept, and in the armies. There are even fome that are compofed of men only : but the people of the court never have recourfe to any but the prince's company.

At eleven o'clock, or about midnight, every one retires but thofe that fup with the Nabob ; who, except on grand feftivals, are always his friends and relations.

This mode of life purfued by Ayder, is, as may be eafily imagined, interrupted in the army. It is likewife occafionally interrupted by hunting parties, by excurfions on foot or horfeback, or by his attending to affift at the exercifes and evolutions made by confiderable bodies of his troops.

When he is obliged to remain a month in camp, or in any town, he ufually goes to the chace twice a week. He hunts the ftag, the roebuck, the antelope, and fometimes the tyger. When notice arrives that this laft animal has been obferved to quit the forefts, and appear in the plain, he mounts his horfe, fol-

lowed

lowed by all his Abyffinians, his fpear-men on foot, and almoft all the nobility armed with fpears and bucklers. The traces of the beaft being found, the hunters furround his hiding place, and contract the circle by degrees. As foon as the creature, who is ufually hid in fome rice ground, perceives his enemies, he roars, and looks every where to find a place of efcape ; and when he prepares to fpring on fome one to force a paffage, he is attacked by Ayder himfelf, to whom the honour of giving the firft ftroke is yielded, and in which he feldom fails. Thus the pleafures of the fovereign are varied to infinity.

THE

TITLES

ASSUMED BY

AYDER ALI KHAN;

WITH THEIR

EXPLICATION.

AYDER ALI KHAN, Nabob Ba-
hader *, Nahondas †, Suba of Scirra,
King of the Canarins and Corgues, Dayva

---

* Nabob Bahader fignifies Incomparable Knight;
the Bahaders in India being what the knights were in
Europe. A great fovereign or general among the
Mogols, after a battle, gives the dignity of Bahader to
a man of diftinction, one of the principal officers
who has behaved with honour. If there has formerly
exifted any ceremony for the creation of a Bahader, it
is now out of ufe : all that is done at prefent is, that the
general publicly praifes his actions, and in his difcourfe
always calls him Bahader ; which title is afterwards
given

va * of Mayſſour, Sovereign of the Empires of Cherequi and Calicut ‡, which contain the kingdoms

given him by all the world indiſcriminately. A Bahader has great privileges : he may go every where completely armed, cauſing a gilt mace to be carried before him, and may appear thus even in the preſence of any ſovereign. When a Bahader arrives at court, he demands an audience, which is always granted : he preſents himſelf with a helmet on, and armed in every other reſpect : the ſovereign ſeeing him enter, riſes and ſalutes him, by embracing twice ; and in converſation uſes the terms *Amaré-Bay*, which ſignify *my brother* ; becauſe all the ſovereigns dignify themſelves with the title of Bahader. Ayder was ſurnamed the Incomparable Bahader ; the true ſignification of the word *Nabob* being *incomparable*; for it is a title of honour, not of dignity : however, by common cuſtom, Nabob of Benguelour is uſed inſtead of Lord or Prince of Benguelour; but literally it only ſignifies incomparable, or without equal, in Benguelour. This title being exclusive, it muſt in no caſe be given to an inferior in preſence of his ſuperior. Ayder, to ſhew that the title of Bahader, which we have rendered Knight, but which literally implies Great Warrior, is above all other titles, ſigns, inſtead of his name, the two letters B. B. for Bahader Bahader.

† Nahondas implies one who is worthy of all the titles of honour.

* Dayva, or regent. It will be hereafter ſeen how Ayder became regent of this kingdom.

‡ Sovereign of the empires of Cherequi and Calicut. The Portugueſe were the firſt Europeans who, arriving with

kingdoms of Cananor, Cochin, Trevancour ; Nabob of Benguelour, Ballapour, Baſſapatnam, or Biſnagar, &c. &c. Lord of the Mountains and Vallies, &c. &c. *, King of the Iſlands of the Sea, &c. &c. †.

with their ſhips on the coaſt of Malabar, gave the title of Emperors to the ſovereigns of theſe two countries. The name anſwers very ill to the power and extent of the ſtates of Cherequi and Samorin.   The only reſemblance they have to emperors is, that they are the chiefs or heads of two confederations of petty princes, or Rajas, to whom the Portugueſe gave the title of Kings, becauſe they have a diadem and purple mantle, having the head wrapped in red muſlin, and a ſtripe of gold faſtened to the back of their head ; and wearing no other clothes than a kind of ſhirt of red gauze or muſlin, reaching almoſt to their knees. Theſe pretended kings ſeldom poſſeſs a territory of more than two, or ſix leagues at the extreme.   They go on foot with their legs naked, followed by their couriers barefoot, and armed with ſabres and bucklers.

    * Ayder is Lord of Malleaur or Carnate ; which two words, in different languages, imply, The Country of Mountains and Vallies.

    † We ſhall hereafter ſhew how this title of King of the Iſles of the Sea was given, when his fleet made the conqueſt of the Maldives, which are ſaid to be twelve thouſand in number.

THE

HISTORY

OF

AYDER ALI KHAN;

OR,

NEW MEMOIRS

CONCERNING

THE EAST INDIES.

AYDER Ali Khan, fon of Nadim Saeb, general of ten thoufand horfe * in the army of the empire, was born in 1728 at Divanelli, a fmall fortrefs or caftle between

---

* General of ten thoufand horfe is nearly the fame as lieutenant-general in France. In the army of the Mogols, all the degrees are conferred by patents, that give power and commiffion to raife ten thoufand men

between Colar and Oscota, in the country of Benguelour. This land was given in fief to his father, who was particularly attached to Nizam El Moulouc, Grand Visir and Suba of Decan.

After the death of Nizam El Moulouc, Nadim Saeb retired to Divanelli with his two sons, Ismael Saeb, and Ayder. Ismael Saeb was much older than his brother. He entered into the service of the king of Mayssour; and in a short time became his first general. The king of Mayssour, as a reward for a victory he had obtained over the Marattas, gave him the country and fortress of Benguelour; which put him into a situation of having a body of troops of his own, that composed part of the

for the service of the empire; with the prerogative to name all the inferior officers, to keep them in discipline, and to distribute justice among them. As the cavalry is the most esteemed service, the degree of general of ten thousand horse is the highest. This general has the right to cause any number of banners or streamers to be carried before him, and to cause a large square standard to be hoisted before his tent, which is, at the same time, a mark of his jurisdiction. A general, or commander in chief, causes two to be hoisted. When the grand army of a Subaship is assembled, a large triangular standard is displayed at the head of the camp.

2

army

army of the king of Mayſſour, when Nazerzing made a deſcent upon the coaſt of Coromandel in 1750. Ayder, then about twenty-
one or twenty-two years old, had never quitted his father's houſe. His father gave him
the command of the quota of troops he was
bound to furniſh to the army of the Suba, for
his lordſhip of Divanelli. It conſiſted only of
fifty horſemen, and two hundred Peadars, or
ſoldiers armed with matchlocks. Ibrahim Saeb,
the maternal uncle of Ayder, ſerved him inſtead of a Mentor.

Ayder being at the battle where Nazerzing
was ſlain, the bravery of the French, who,
to the number of eight hundred, ſeconded by
four thouſand Seapoys, had the courage to attack the army of the Mogols, then more than
three hundred thouſand ſtrong, made ſuch an
impreſſion on his mind, that he was perſuaded the French were capable of undertaking
the moſt difficult enterprizes. Having followed Mouzaferzing, ſucceſſor to Nazerzing,
to Pondicherry, the obſervations he made in
that city, upon the manners, diſcipline, fortifications, buildings, arts, and induſtry of
the French, gave him the higheſt eſteem for
that celebrated and warlike nation, and more

E 2 eſpecially

especially for M. Dupleix, who was then governor.

In 1751, Mouzaferzing having withdrawn his army to Golconda, Ayder, whose father was dead, went to join his brother in Mayssour. On the account the young man gave of the advantageous arms of the Europeans, and their address in managing great guns, Ismael Saeb dispatched a Guebre to Bombay, to purchase cannon, and musquets with bayonets.— This Persian, who died in 1767, purchased two thousand musquets, and six pieces of cannon, of the governor of Bombay. He likewise enrolled thirty European sailors, of different nations, that he collected on the coast of Malabar, to serve as canoniers.

Ismael Saeb, brother to Ayder, was thus the first Indian who formed a corps of Seapoys armed with firelocks and bayonets, and who had a train of artillery served by Europeans. This procured him new advantages over the enemies of the king of Mayssour, and increased the esteem and friendship of that prince for him.

Nand Raja, brother to the king of Mayssour, and Dayva *, having formed an army

to

---

* Nand Raja was Dayva, which signifies regent, as
Ayder

to make a defcent upon the coaft of Coromandel, and join that of the Englifh, Ayder, at the recommendation of his brother, obtained the command of the cavalry of this army. The Englifh, aided by the Mayffourians, forced the French troops, combined with thofe of Chanda Saeb, to furrender themfelves prifoners of war, and to give up the Pagod of Schirnigam, in which they had taken refuge. It was on this occafion that Chanda Saeb was made prifoner. Nand Raja afterwards quarrelling with the Englifh, M. Dupleix formed an alliance with him; and it was agreed to lay fiege to Trichnapoli, a ftrong place on the river Caveri, with an army compofed of French forces, together with thofe of Mayffour, and thofe of Chanda Saeb *, Nabob of Arcot. The Englifh, who were the allies of Mehemet Ali Khan †, competitor of Chanda Saeb, had then a garrifon in Trichnapoli.

When the French fet out from Pondicherry, in 1752, to join Nand Raja, they were har-

Ayder is at prefent. It will hereafter be feen how this prince loft the regency.

* Chanda Saeb, as has been fhewn in the Introduction, was the Nabob acknowledged by the French.

† See the Introduction.

E 3 raffed

raffed in their march by a body of Mahratta
cavalry, commanded by a chief allied with the
Englifh.   On this occafion the commandant
of the French troops wrote to the regent of
Mayffour to fend him a reinforcement.

Ayder was fent to his affiftance, at the head
of eighteen hundred horfe.   It was then that
Ayder began to be known to the French, and
to acquire fome reputation among the Europeans, whence he had his pretended name of
Andernec.   Before that time, the French, the
Englifh, and other European nations, had
very little connection with, or knowledge of,
the interior parts of the country; and there
was not perhaps two Frenchmen at Pondicherry that could converfe in the language of
the Mogols, which is a kind of Perfian, and
is commonly called Moors.   The officers and
foldiers had no other interpreters than their
Dabafhis, or Malabar domeftics, who knew
only their own language and a fort of corrupt
Portuguefe.   The Malabar language, though
very regular, is perhaps the pooreft language
in being : fo that the word *Dore* fignifies
Mr. or Sir ; and to exprefs the word governor,
general, or *the fuperior Sir*, they fay *Peri-dore*,
which is *the great Sir*, or *Mafter :* and, in
the

the fame manner, to denote any chief whatfoever, the Malabar language has only the word
Naic; and they ufe *Tanjaor Naic* to fignify the
king or Raja of Tanjaor; and *Narim Naic*,
and *Chabri Naic*, to denote the ferjeant Narim, or the corporal Chabri: and the name
Ayder Naic implying the chief Ayder, the
French have formed it into Andernec. It is
this name of Naic that has caufed it to be
imagined that Ayder had been a corporal of
Seapoys. He was then called Ayder Saeb,
which is the fame as Mr. Ayder. His name
was enlarged in proportion as his power increafed, as the cuftom is among the Mogols;
and he is now called Ayder Ali Khan.

When the French army had joined that of
Mayffour, Ayder *, whofe camp then formed
the left wing of the Mayffourian army, came
and encamped himfelf to the right of the
French, in fpite of all the arguments of the
French commandant, and the regent of Mayffour; and, however difagreeable it was to the

* M. de Maiffin, who commanded the French at
that time, is the author of this anecdote, which fufficiently confutes the feveral ftories that have been cir-
culated refpecting Ayder's intentions.

French

French to fee themfelves as it were cooped
up, he would not remove from the ftation he
had affumed. He informed the commandant
that he wifhed to be near the French, that he
might learn from them the art of war. In
fact, he was very attentive and exact in ob-
ferving every thing that paffed in the French
camp; and caufed feveral of their evolutions *
to be repeated, as well as was in his power,
in his own camp.—This repetition caufed fome
diverfion to the French officers and foldiers,
whom he was attentive to pleafe by his politenefs and good manners. But it was not with
any fatisfaction they obferved that Ayder had
drawn the moft active and intelligent French
foldiers into his fervice. He had ftill in his
fervice, in 1770, the Sicur Stenet †, fon of a
Cent-Suiffe of Verfaiiles, who was a volun-
teer at the fiege of Trichnapoli in 1753: he
took him at that time into his fervice, and
fent him to his brother in Mayffour, as he did
every other Frenchman that chofe to engage
in his fervice. Thefe enrollments were made

---

* Ayder, though general of cavalry in the army of
Mayffour, had troops of his own.—The left is the poft
of honour in India.

† He was then captain in the artillery.

with

with fome dexterity ; and, as there was need of his fervices, the French commandant winked at the irregularity of the proceeding.

General Lawrence, who was then only major, attempting to throw fome fuccours and a convoy into Trichnapoli, received a confiderable check ; of which, in his Memoirs, he gives all the honour to Ayder and his cavalry. Englifh jealoufy perhaps induced him to diminifh the merit of the French ; but it is certain that Ayder diftinguifhed himfelf highly on this occafion.

In 1755, Nand Raja * having quitted the French to return to Mayffour, Ayder made a particular treaty with M. Dupleix, by which he engaged to remain with his troops, forming a body of fix thoufand men, till the capture of Trichnapoli ; and he did not return to Mayffour till Mr. Godehen, fucceffor to M. Dupleix, had made a truce with the Englifh, and given orders to raife the fiege of Trichnapoli. In 1756, Ayder being informed

* The caufe of the retreat of Nand Raja with the army of Mayffour, was, that M. de Buffi, with a body of French, had accompanied Salaberzing, Suba of Decan, when he came to Syringpatnam, capital of Mayffour, and exacted contributions.

of

of the death of his brother, as he was on his way to rejoin him, haftened to receive the fucceffion that had devolved to him by the law ; his brother having no male children. This death put him in poffeffion of a handfome fortrefs, a fertile territory, and a body of troops, which, joined to his own, amounted to above fifteen thoufand men, including two hundred Europeans, and three thoufand of excellent cavalry. The king of Mayffour having the fame confidence in him as his brother Ifmael, appointed him generaliffimo of his army.

The kings of Mayffour being Bramins, had united the royal dignity and the priefthood ; and, to be more venerable in the eyes of their people, they affected to appear in public only twice a year ; namely, on thofe days when they prefided at the folemn ceremonies of their religion. And in order to appear folely occupied with the facred myfteries, which they celebrated with pomp and magnificence, they abandoned the government to a Dayva, or regent, who, till the time of Nand Raja, had always been one of the king's neareft relations. But a Bramin, named Canero, favourite of this prince, perfuaded him to affume the

government

government himfelf, and forfake his brother Nand Raja. This laft, who had neither the capacity nor the application, nor even the firm-nefs, neceffary to fupport himfelf in this dignity, made no refiftance; and preferred banifh-ment to the frontier to the hazard of making the leaft remonftrance.

Canero having taken entire poffeffion of the mind of the king, was declared his minifter, and charged with the adminiftration of affairs. Ayder kept his command of the army.

The power, the reputation, and the love of the foldiery that were poffeffed by Ayder, ought to have fecured him from the envy and jealoufy of this ambitious minifter : but Canero, facri-ficing every thing to thofe paffions, ventured even to make a private treaty with the Marat-tas, enemies of the ftate. In confequence of this treaty, the Maratta army entered Mayflour in the rainy feafon, at the moment when Ayder leaft expected them, and, deceived by Canero, had difperfed his troops.

The approach of the Marattas, and their fu-periority in number, obliged him to advance towards Syringpatnam, capital of the king-dom, that offered him a fure afylum in the ifland on which the city is fituated, and which

cannot

cannot be entered, when the Caveri is fwelled by the rains, but by the bridge of Syringpatnam.

Canero, who, in another fituation, would have done his utmoſt to have prevented Ayder from entering the royal city, preſſed him to pitch his camp on the iſland. Ayder fell into the fnare of the perfidious Bramin. He paſſed the bridge and went through the town with his army, which he encamped at the oppoſite extremity of the iſland. The Maratta army foon appeared, and inveſted that part of the river, where it is fordable in the uſual ſtate of the waters.

Ayder, having no fuſpicion of the treachery of Canero, depended on the well-furniſhed magazines of the city for the fubfiftence of his troops. But he was in the higheſt aſtoniſhment, the day after the arrival of the Marattas, when he beheld the gates of the city ſhut ; and was informed that Canero had determined that the whole army ſhould periſh, either by hunger or the cannon of the city, unleſs they delivered up Ayder to the king, who had ſtrong reaſons for fecuring his perſon. This account convinced Ayder that Canero had fworn his deſtruction. He ſent ſeveral officers to treat

with

with him; but the day was confumed without effect. When the night was clofed in, he fent for the chiefs of the different corps into his tent. He thanked them for their fidelity to him, and affured them that he would not be the caufe of the lofs of fo many brave men. He advifed them to arrange their affairs, at the break of day, as well as they could, with Canero; and informed them that he fhould determine for himfelf in the courfe of that very night. At the fame time he gave fix months pay and gratification to the whole army, which was diftributed to the foldiers before any treaty was made with Canero. He then embraced the principal officers, telling them that he depended on their friendfhip when a favourable opportunity might arrive; and afterwards difmiffed them. About midnight, affembling thirty of his men on whofe fidelity and bravery he could rely, he committed a quantity of gold to the charge of each; and, putting himfelf at their head, attempted to pafs the river by fwimming. He fucceeded; and happily eluding the Maratta army, kept a direct courfe, without ftopping, till he arrived at Benguelour, which is thirty leagues diftant from Syringpatnam.

3

When

When he came near this fortrefs, he fent one of his friends to his uncle Ibrahim Saeb, to whom he had entrufted the government, to inform him, that though he had formerly poffeffed lands, fortreffes, treafures, and an army, he had now no more remaining than thirty friends, who were determined to fhare his fortune ; that he therefore begged him to fay, with fincerity, whether he could ftill rely on his friendfhip ; and that his anfwer would determine whether he fhould come to Benguelour, or feek an afylum elfewhere. His uncle having received this meffage, mounted his horfe, and returned with the meffenger of Ayder. " Courage !" faid he, on meeting his nephew, " nothing is loft that you have trufted in my hands ; and God will affift you to recover the reft." Ayder embraced him, and they entered Benguelour.

Seeing himfelf thus in poffeffion of a ftrong place, he began to hope for the re-eftablifhment of his affairs ; and his wifhes were foon partly realized, by the unforefeen arrival of almoft all his cavalry, which the brave Moctum Saeb, his brother-in-law, brought after him.

At the time that Canero was in treaty with the chiefs of Ayder's army, Moctum feizing
the

the inftant of a fudden and unexpected decreafe
of the Caveri, croffed the river at the head of
three thoufand horfe; and overthrowing every
force the Marattas brought to oppofe him, he
opened a paffage, and arrived at Benguelour by
favour of the woods and mountains he was perfectly acquainted with, having loft a very inconfiderable number of men.

Ayder made ufe of every refource. He raifed
troops with the utmoft celerity; and being neceffarily on the defenfive, he began a war of
ftratagem with the Marattas, feconded by his
brother-in-law, and affifted by the nature of
the country.

In the year 1760, at the time he was bufied
in defending his own proper home, Pondicherry being in great danger, he detached feven
thoufand men, at the requeft of Mr. Lally, to
affift the French, under the command of his
brother-in-law Moctum.

Moctum, in his way to Pondicherry, placed a
garrifon in the fortrefs of Thiagar, which the
Sieur Mariol put into his hands, by order of
Mr. Lally; and the garrifon of that place, confifting of three hundred French and twelve hundred feapoys, having joined the army of Ayder,
Moctum, after repelling a party of the Englifh,

lifh, who pretended to difpute the paffage of a river, encamped on the glacis of Pondicherry, where he remained two months ; and threw feveral convoys into the place, without being able to prevail on M. Lally to encamp without the town. He returned to Ayder, bringing with him all the French cavalry under the Sieurs Alain and Hughel, and fuch workmen as were at Pondicherry : a precious acquifition, which has highly contributed to the fuccefs of Ayder, by furnifhing him with fkilful armourers, carpenters, and other workmen from the arfenal of Pondicherry, collected with much expence and trouble by the French. Moctum, in his return, paffing by Thiagar, withdrew his garrifon; and the French replaced fome feapoys in the fame : Moctum faying, with a generous fpirit of integrity, that as the place was to have been the reward for delivering Pondicherry, juftice required him to reftore it, fince he had failed in the attempt.

This action, however, may perhaps have been more political than generous. But the fact is, that Thiagar was not furrendered to the Englifh till after the capture of Pondicherry.

During

During the abfence of Moctum, Ayder made a truce with the Marattas, a nation very averfe to long wars. This Nabob, efteeming the French in the higheft degree, faw with great fatisfaction a fine corps of cavalry of that nation in his army; and he was ftill more re-joiced to behold them accompanied by a body of workmen, for want of whofe affiftance he was in no fmall diftrefs. His brother-in-law, who had conciliated the affection of all who knew him, was doubtlefs entitled to the moft honourable reception. Ayder, on the con-trary, received him with coolnefs, and even with indignation; making it a crime that he had not accomplifhed the object of his mif-fion, by raifing the fiege of Pondicherry; and, without waiting for his reply, he degraded him to the rank of fimple cavalier, as being unworthy of any command. This treatment, which aftonifhed all the world, was highly mortifying to the officers and foldiers who had borne a part in the expedition. Many of them, particularly the French, fpoke to Ayder in favour of his brother-in-law; but he ap-pearing always in anger, but at the fame time willing to do juftice, confented to affemble all the chiefs of his army, and allowed the friends of Moctum to give a detail of his conduct during the expedition to Pondicherry. The whole assembly unanimously extolling the merit of Moctum, Ayder ordered his grand savari * to be immediately prepared ; and being on his march to the house of his brother-in-law, followed by the whole assembly, he met him in the † bazar, where he was walking on foot like a common soldier. As soon as Ayder saw him, he descended from his elephant, approached Moctum and embraced him cordially several times, and addressed him nearly in these words : " I find, " by the account of your friends, that I was " wrong in blaming your conduct, and was " going to your house to make an apology " for my error. I am happy that I have met " you, that the satisfaction I make may be " the more public." Then causing him to mount the king's own elephant, he conducted

---

* *Savari* is a word that signifies the grand retinue of the sovereign on occasions of ceremony. It will be described in a future part of this work.

† The bazar is that part of a city or camp where the shops of the merchants are situate. The streets of the bazar being usually covered, it is common to walk there.

· him

him to his own houfe, riding before him on horfeback, with all his attendants in procef-fion, and followed by the people and foldiery ; who, happy at the reconciliation of Ayder with Mo&tum, fang his praifes, in which his brother-in-law was not forgotten.

The condu&t of Ayder in this tranfa&ion was founded in juftice ; but, according to all appearance, it was not lefs the effe&t of policy. He was then looking forward at a great for-tune, and was defirous of convincing his offi-cers, that, as he had not fpared his brother-in-law, who was his deareft friend, he fhould not fail in punifhing any negle&t of duty in them.

Ayder loft no time in turning the arrival of the French to his advantage. He fpread the news by his emiffaries, magnifying their number ; and, avowing his intention to march to Syringpatnam, he invited all the great men of Mayffour to join him for the purpofe of de-livering the king from the power of the trea-cherous Canero, and to reftore the govern-ment in conformity to the laws of the king-dom. Nand Raja, who had always held a fecret correfpondence with Ayder, quitted his exile and joined him ; and it is faid, that

F 2   he

he furnifhed him with large fums of money to raife troops and increafe his army.

Canero, knowing the activity of Ayder, was not remifs in his preparations. He collected an army vaftly more numerous than that of Ayder; and, by virtue of careffes and rewards, gained to his party thofe Europeans who had managed the artillery of Ayder before his flight. His artillery was, befides, far fuperior in number and quality, fo that he did not fear to go out of the town, and waited for Ayder at Cenapatnam, an open village feven leagues diftant from Syringpatnam.

The two armies were encamped at the diftance of three leagues afunder. The dependence of Ayder on his own troops, and hopes he had been encouraged to form from his French fuccours, did not prevent his employing ftratagem againft his enemy. Succefs attended his attempts.

There was a lady at Syringpatnam, commonly called the old Dayva, becaufe her hufband, brother of the king and of Nand Raja, had been regent or Dayva of the kingdom.

This lady had poffeffed great power during the regency of her hufband, who left her extremely

tremely rich. Nand Raja, her brother-in-law, on his acceffion to the regency, had not that refpect and confideration fhe thought were due to her : from that moment fhe declared herfelf his enemy, and contributed much to his lofs of the regency. This princefs had always protected Ayder and his brother; and, as her conduct was not very exemplary, the fcandalous chronicle affirmed, that Ayder and his brother fhared her private favours. Though diftant from Syringpatnam, Ayder had always kept up an intimate correfpondence with this lady, who was not a friend to Canero, though apparently, from policy, much attached to him. On the affurance that Ayder gave her, that Nand Raja fhould never be regent, fhe promifed to ferve him to the utmoft of her power, and even fupplied him with large fums of money.

Ayder, to make every advantage of the friendfhip of this lady, on whom he had an entire reliance, tranfmitted to her fictitious letters, addreffed to the principal heads of the army of Canero, in which he appeared to prefcribe, in confequence of an agreement long eftablifhed, operations to be made by them upon certain fignals appointed by Ayder. The intention of thefe

F 3 manœuvres

manœuvres was apparently that of furround-
ing Canero at the commencement of the battle, and preventing his efcape. The lady
having received thefe letters, repaired to the
camp of Canero the night preceding the
battle: fhe gave him the letters; and, by an
artful converfation on the bufinefs, increafed
the confternation of the minifter : the confequence was, that he immediately retired to
Syringpatnam, leaving the command of the
army to an old general named Pirkhan, whom
he believed to be in his interefts, but who
was really the friend of Ayder.

Ayder, informed of every thing as it happened, marched with his army at the break of
day to approach that of Canero, thrown into great agitation by his departure. The news
of this precipitate march augmented the confufion, and the general was by no means defirous
of removing it. A number of deferters from
Canero's army arrived in the camp of Ayder,
with the news of his flight. As foon as that
Nabob heard their report, he caufed his army
to halt, and fent a meffenger to the general of
the other army to propofe a conference, publicly affuring him, that his exertions were directed againft the traitor Canero, and not
the king and kingdom of Mayffour. Pirkhan,
after

after taking the advice of the principal chiefs of his army, confented to a conference with Ayder and Nand Raja, in the prefence of the two armies; when it was refolved, to the great fatisfaction of the foldiers, that they fhould unite, and form but one army; and that a deputation fhould be fent immediately to the king of Mayffour, praying him to drive the traitor Canero out of the kingdom, as a declared enemy of the king and the ftate. When the two armies were united, Ayder, to the furprife of every one, commanded before him the Europeans who had formerly been attached to his fervice and that of his brother: he made them ground their arms, and, giving every one a ftroke, after the manner of the Indians, when they difhonour or degrade any one, he drove them out of his camp. He was induced to this feverity, as he faid, becaufe thefe foldiers, having been loaded with favours by his brother and himfelf, were the only men of all his troops who had prefumed to carry arms againft him. The French cavalry from Pondicherry were prefent at this execution, and pretended to approve it.

The deputation from the army being arrived at Syringpatnam, the anfwer of the king,

dictated,

dictated, no doubt, by Canero, was, that they were traitors, and that the king would punish them. On this anfwer, it was refolved to lay fiege to Syringpatnam ; which was immediately done, to prevent Canero from calling in the affiftance of the Marattas.

The inhabitants of the city had no fooner heard the report of a few cannon, than they affembled, and remonftrated in ftrong terms againft Canero, excited, moft probably, by the dowager Dayva ; who at length prevailed on the king to deliver Canero to the army, and to declare Ayder regent inftead of Nand Raja, who expected the appointment, and fuppofed Ayder would be contented with the poft of generaliffimo.

Upon his accepting the regency, Ayder made every fubmiffion to appeafe Nand Raja. He gave him a confiderable territory, and made a promife, both in writing and by oath, that he would never make any attempt on his liberty, property, or life, but would always regard him as his father.

Ayder afterwards caufed the Bramin doctors to be affembled to judge Canero. He was condemned to death for having invited a foreign enemy into the kingdom, and levying

war

war againſt the king's moſt faithful ſubjects.
By virtue of his power as regent, Ayder ſpared
his life, and commuted his puniſhment into
that of being ſhut up in an iron cage in the
middle of the moſt public place of Benguelour.; where it is ſtill to be ſeen, with the
bones of this unhappy favourite, who lived two
years in the cage, expoſed to the inſults of a
populace that adored Ayder.

As a beginning of his performance of the
duty of a regent, Ayder cauſed an exact account to be made out of the royal revenues, together with the treaſure and jewels. He found
that the greateſt part of the jewels, inſtead of
being in the treaſury, were in pawn with the
court banker *, who had advanced money
when

---

* In every great city of 'Indoſtan, eſpecially thoſe
where courts are kept, there are rich bankers, named Sar-
cars. They are all Guzerats, or natives of that country. Their integrity or credit, as well as their ſkill
in buſineſs, is much eſteemed. Their buſineſs is properly
that of bankers, borrowing or lending money, furniſhing
or taking letters of exchange on all places, not excepting even thoſe at which they have no correſpon-
dence. In this laſt caſe, they make uſe of money
porters, who carry money to any diſtance, charging
their carriage at per league. Theſe men may be depended on; and it is related, that one of them having

when Salabetzing, Suba of Decan, accompanied by M. Buffi, came as far as the gates of Syringpatnam, and forced the king of Mayffour
to pay contributions.

Ayder being informed that this man had
acquired the whole of his immenfe fortune in
the fervice of the ftate, was difpleafed that he
had demanded pledges on lending money to the
government.   He ordered the jewels to be

ing carried off a confiderable fum belonging to a banker
at Madras, the reft of the people following the fame
occupation affembled, and reimburfed the banker, tho'
under no obligation to do it; and two of them immediately repaired to Goa, where the thief had taken refuge, and, cutting off his head, brought it to Madras,
where it was carried to all the bankers to be feen, in
order that the punifhment of the crime might enfure a
continuation of their confidence.   Letters of exchange
are far more ancient in India than in Europe; but are
not drawn to order, which creates a difficulty in cafe
of the death or abfence of the perfon in whofe favour
they are drawn.   This difficulty is in fome meafure
obviated by naming feveral perfons in the fame bill :
fo that the letter of exchange drawn by an Indian
banker runs, "Pay to John, or in his abfence to Pe-
ter, or in his abfence to James, &c."

Befides dealing in money, thefe bankers traffic likewife in precious ftones, coral, pearls, and gold and filver plate.   Some of them are very rich; and there
are infurance companies of great credit at Surat, at
Madras, and at Calcutta, entirely compofed of Guzerat
bankers.

taken

taken out of his hands, and his due paid him ; but at the fame time nominated a commiffion to infpect his accounts. The commiffioners having found him guilty of fraud and extortion in his dealings with the ftate, condemned him to perpetual imprifonment and confifcation of all his property. The luxury of this banker was enormous. It is faid that his children had cradles of gold fufpended from the ceiling by chains of the fame metal. Ayder caufed the judgment to be put in execution, but gave him a penfion to fubfift on ; and placed his fons in the fervice, where they have been preferred.

Order and regularity were foon eftablifhed in the finances, and Ayder then proceeded to compel a number of petty tyrants, known by the name of Palleagars *, to evacuate their fortreffes. He was under the neceffity of ufing force with fome of them, but the greater part treated with him in a friendly manner. He compelled likewife many Rajas, vaffals and tributaries to the kingdom of Mayffour, to

* The Palleagars are people who inhabit caftles or fmall fortreffes. There are many in India, but there does not exift one in all the dominions of Ayder. This name is given only to Gentoos, and is not properly applied to Mogels.

acknow-

acknowledge their dependence, and pay the tribute with punctuality and exactnefs. He likewife obliged many neighbouring kings, fuch as the kings of Canara, the Marattas, and the Patane Nabobs of Canour, Carpet, and Sanour, to reftore the lands they had ufurped from the kingdom of Mayffour. But he did not accomplifh all this without declaring war, and obtaining many victories over them. The Patanes were dreaded through all Indoftan, for their valour and their perfidy. Ayder acquired great reputation by the fignal victory he gained over the three Nabobs, near Sanour; for which he was indebted to the bravery and fpirited evolutions of the French cavalry under M. Hughel.

This victory of Sanour induced Bazaletzing, king of Adonis, and brother of Nizam Ali Khan, Suba of Decan, to fend an embaffy to him.

Thofe princes were at war with the Marattas, who had lately received a confiderable check on the banks of the Kifna, in a battle they had loft againft the united armies of the Grand Vifir * of the empire, and of Abdalla, king

* This Grand Vifir was Sha Abadin Khan, or
otherwife

king of the Patanes †, in which ſixty thouſand Marattas were left on the ſpot.

Bazaletzing had laid ſiege to Scirra, a ſtrong place ſituated between his dominions and the kingdom of Mayſſour, and gives the title to a Subaſhip; of which the whole diſtrict has been either ſeized by the Marattas, or united to the Subaſhip of Decan. This prince imagined, that taking advantage of the defeat of the Marattas, he ſhould eaſily get poſſeſſion of Scirra, and,

otherwiſe named Suja Dowla, who ſucceeded his grandfather Nizam El Moulouc, and his father Grou‐zeddy Khan.—He is, beſides, ſovereign of an extenſive territory on the Ganges.

† This Abdallah is king of Candahar. When he had joined his army to that of Suja Dowla, they drove the Marattas from Delhi as far as Kiſna, where the fugitives croſſed the river, and waited to defend the paſſage. The Patanes and the Mogols ſeveral times attempted to croſs the river, but could not ſucceed, many Patanes being taken priſoners in the attempt. Raguba, general of the Marattas, cauſed them to be brought before him, and propoſed to them to join the Marattas. They replied, that Mahometans were not made to ſerve, but to command other men. Raguba demanded, if they were ſtronger or more courageous than other men? To which they replied, Give us arms, and you ſhall ſee. As they were very few in number, Raguba cauſed arms to be given them; and they inſtantly fell upon the Marattas, who were obli‐
ged

and, by that means, become of equal rank with his brother, by acquiring the title of Suba. But, his army not being equal to the undertaking, he experienced a refiftance that would have reduced him to the fhameful neceffity of raifing the fiege, if he had not been advifed to form an alliance with Ayder; who was enchanted to find himfelf fought after by a prince of fo elevated a rank. He did not, however, confent to join his army till he had previoufly made an advantageous treaty. In

ged to put them all to the fword. Abdalla and Suja Dowla, finding too much difficulty in forcing a paffage over the Kifna, made ufe of ftratagem. They pretended to quarrel, and Abdalla departed, as if intending to return to his own dominions. Raguba, being advifed of this, paffed the Kifna to attack Suja Dowla, who pretended to avoid him; but, fending intelligence to Abdalla, the two allies joined, and faced their enemy. The Marattas were attacked, and gave way; and, being vigoroufly followed, they loft fixty thoufand men, for want of time to repafs the Kifna. Raguba was general only for the minority of Madurao, his nephew, whom he caufed to be affaffinated. The Marattas did not fuffer him to retain the regency during the minority of the fon of Madurao, but expelled him. He took refuge among the Englifh at Bombay, who efpoufed his caufe. This is precifely the event that occafioned the war between the Marattas and that European nation.

this

this treaty it was agreed, that Ayder fhould appear before Scirra with his army, and a numerous artillery; that Bazaletzing and himfelf fhould carry on the fiege conjointly, till the place was taken; that as foon as it fhould furrender, each army fhould take poffeffion on its refpective fide of attack; that all the artillery, ammunition, and in general every thing that could be carried away, fhould be the fhare of Bazaletzing, who fhould either take it in kind, or receive the value from Ayder; and, that this laft fhould take poffeffion of the place.

Ayder being arrived before the place with a well-difciplined army, and a grand train of artillery ferved by Europeans, made his attack in a manner very different from that made ufe of by Bazaletzing. By fuccefsful undermining, he blew up two baftions and the curtain, which forced the befieged to furrender at difcretion, and increafed the terror his arms had fpread over the extenfive empire of India.

In the execution of the treaty between thefe two princes, Bazaletzing, who was always afterwards called the Merchant by Ayder, preferred the receiving money for his fhare of the capture; and befides, engaged to folicit his

brothers,

brothers, the Grand Vifir, and the Suba of
Decan, to caufe Ayder to be acknowledged
Suba of Scirra, which immediately took effect, the Grand Vifir * fending him an embaffy with the Paravana which declared him
Suba of Scirra, with all the honours annexed to the title, as the round palanquin †,
the fifhes head, &c. It was thus that Ayder,
born a private perfon, found himfelf raifed to
the rank of the greateft princes of India ‡;
and, from a fubject of the king of Mayffour,
he became his fuperior; the kingdom of Mayffour, which is held of the Mogol emperor,

---

* The Mogol empire was then in a ftate of anarchy,
the emperor being no more than an ineffectual name.
Allumfha, one of the princes of the Mogol blood, had
retired to Ilha Hadabad, where he affumed the title of
Great Mogol ; but Suja Dowla acknowledged another
young prince, then an infant. His uncles Nizam Dowla, Suba of Decan, Bazaletzing, king of Adonis, and
Ayder by complaifance for Sujah Dowla, acknowledged the fame prince, but merely by name, without
rendering any obedience or fubmiffion to either him or
his vifir, who was prefumed to have the regency.

† Thefe honours are marks of the dignity of Suba,
and will be explained in a future page.

‡ The Subas are at prefent the greateft princes in
India, and regard themfelves as the reprefentatives of
the emperor. They are above the tributary kings of
the empire.

having

having been comprized in his Subaſhip.   At the time of his receiving the title and honours of Suba of Scirra, he engaged to make war on the Marattas ; who had then ſeen the end of their empire, if the princes, ſons of Nizam El Moulouc, had poſſeſſed as much courage and intelligence as Ayder ; and if, more eſpe-cially, the king of the Patanes had not aban-doned his allies, and returned into his own country, ſatisfied with the immenſe plunder he had obtained.

Ayder, continuing the war with ſucceſs againſt the Marattas, took Markſira and Mag-gheri, ſtrong places in the diſtrict of Scirra, as well as the kingdom of Biſnagar or Baſſa-patnam.   But the Marattas having collected their forces againſt him, he, by the puſillani-mity of his allies, had nearly loſt his life, having received a ſtroke on the head with a ſabre, in a battle in which neither ſide gained the victory.   A few days afterwards he con-cluded a truce for three years ; and preſerved his conqueſts by paying a ſum of money to the general of that nation.

This war was ſcarcely finiſhed, when a new opportunity preſented itſelf for extending the power and reputation of Ayder.   The ſon of the queen of Canara had efcaped from Rana Biddeluru, capital of that kingdom, and came to the Suba at Bifnagar, to implore his affiftance, that his mother might be compelled to put him in poffeffion of the kingdom of his anceftors; the regency of which fhe had held fince the death of her hufband, the late king, and father of the young prince, and ftill retained it, though her fon had arrived at the age prefcribed by law for him to take charge of the government himfelf.

As the kingdom of Canara was comprized in the fubafhip of Scirra, the prince could carry his complaint with propriety to no other tribunal than that of Ayder. The young prince was therefore favourably received, and his mother was cited, by an ambaffador of Ayder, to appear before the Suba at a time fixed.

This woman, who poffeffed a degree of courage unufual in her fex, and who, from the anarchy that had long reigned in the Mogol's empire, was habituated to defpife the orders of the emperor and his officers, replied to the ambaffador of Ayder, that fhe was queen, and knew no fuperior. On this anfwer, which Ayder expected, war was determined on againft the queen; but the nature of the country promifed

mifed to throw many difficulties in the way of the expedition.

Rana Biddeluru, capital of the kingdom of Canara, is one of the largeft and beft peopled cities of India. It contains at leaft fifty thoufand fouls ; among whom are about thirty thoufand Chriftians, who have great privileges. This confiderable population is, however, by no means proportionate to the extent of the city, whofe circuit exceeds three leagues. It will not be found that this is an exaggeration, when it is confidered, that there are ftreets in it, nearly in a right line, of two leagues in length. Befides, the greateft part of the ground on which the town ftands is inhabited by great men and nobility, whofe houfes are each in the midft of a large garden, enclofing vaft bafons or refervoirs of water, as well for the purpofes of pleafure as utility. A prodigious number of trees, planted in thefe gardens, fhade all the ftreets ; which are watered on each fide by a rivulet of clear and limpid water, and have no other pavement than a fine gravel.

This beautiful city is fituated near a fmall mountain, at whofe fummit is a confiderable fortrefs, fince much more ftrongly fortified

G 2   by

by Ayder. The mountain is in a plain about five or fix leagues in diameter, environed by mountains and forefts that extend for more than twenty leagues every way, and are not to be paffed but by narrow paffages, defended by forts at a fmall diftance from each other. Thefe circumftances render the accefs to the city extremely difficult for an army, that may be checked at every ftep by an inconfiderable force, and cannot encamp but in the length of a ftony paffage, where it is liable to be attacked by the people of the country, who know all the fecret paffages, and can continually lay in ambufh to annoy their enemy. The woods cannot be cut down, much lefs burned*, without infinite labour ; and they are filled with tygers, bears, elephants, and every fpecies of venomous reptiles.

A mafs of fuch almoft infuperable obftacles as prefented themfelves to Ayder, ought to have deterred him from his enterprize, if he had not been accompanied by the young prince, who was beloved by the people and the men in power ; while the queen his mother

---

* In thefe forefts are a prodigious number of bamboos, a tree that cannot be burned without firft cutting it down and drying it.

was

was detested by them, as well for her haugh-
tiness and pride, as for having contracted a
second marriage with a Bramin, contrary to
the law of the place, which prohibits the
widows of their kings from marrying a second
time.

Ayder, determined to make the attempt, left
Bisnagar, carrying with him the prince of
Canara, at the head of 6,000 men of his best
cavalry, and some Caleros, men habituated to
traverse the mountains and forests. He was
followed by a number of oxen * loaded with
rice; and with no other baggage, he advanced,
by forced marches, towards the capital of
Canara. His movement was so rapid, that he
passed on without finding any obstacle, and

---

* Oxen are of the greatest utility in India, both
for draught and carriage. This species, which is
but little varied in Europe, is very much so in India, much more than any other species of animals.
There are some extremely tall, some middle sized, and
some small. They work at the plough, draw all sorts
of carriages, and go very fast. Some have their horns
strait, others curved, and others have none at all. The
greater number have a bunch on the back; and generally it is an animal of the greatest utility, which is
still more enhanced by the consideration, that after doing much service, its flesh is eatable, and its skin tanned
for leather.

arrived

arrived on the plain of Biddeluru before the queen had received any news of his march.. His cavalry, accuftomed to every kind of. ground, terrified the Canarins, who had never beheld a legion of that kind. The good difcipline obferved by his troops, and the fight of the legitimate prince, caufed Ayder to be received every where as a tutelar divinity.

On his appearance in the plain, his cavalry eafily difperfed a part of the queen's army, that attempted to oppofe his paffage ; and that princefs, who had fcarcely time to make her efcape, was purfued, taken, and conducted into the prefence of the conqueror.

Ayder ufed his victory with the greateft moderation. He received the queen in the moft gracious manner, and reconciled her with her fon ; who granted her a confiderable penfion, allowing her to live with her hufband. To fatisfy the people, who ardently defired it, the young prince was proclaimed king : he made homage to the empire for his kingdom, and figned the treaty, as well as his mother, and the principal great men of the country.

While thefe tranfactions were performing in the kingdom of Canara, the army of Ayder advanced into the country, and his infantry

took

took poffeffion, without refiftance, of all the pofts that were neceffary to fecure his return, and the fuccefs of any thing he might think proper to undertake.

Before he engaged in the war that was to place the prince of Canara on the throne of his anceftors, Ayder made a treaty with him, by which the prince yielded to the Suba the port of Mangalor, with a tract of country to form a communication from thence to the frontiers of the kingdom of Mayffour. In execution of this treaty, Ayder, after caufing the new king to be crowned, marched with a party of his troops to take poffeffion of Mangalor, leaving a part of his army encamped at the gates of Rana Biddeluru.

The queen of Canara, enraged to find herfelf deprived of the fovereignty, had pretended to be reconciled with her fon, and to acknowledge him as king, with no other intention than to wait for an opportunity of deftroying Ayder. With this hope, and completely to gratify her vengeance, fhe refolved on the death of this generous Suba. She therefore endeavoured to gain the confidence of her fon, whofe feeble and pufillanimous fpirit fhe well knew. She reproached him, with a diffembled

G 4. tendernefs,

tendernefs, that, to haften the beginning of his reign, he had inconfiderately delivered up his kingdom to barbarians, the enemies of his religion, who would leave him only the empty name of king, after depriving him of the moft valuable part of his dominions, and moft probably would finifh by entirely robbing him of the whole. At length, by force of infinuations, and under the appearance of a highly difinterefted perfon, who had refigned a kingdom to him, fhe fucceeded in her endeavours to make him regret the treaty with Ayder ; and, continuing to act on his fears of the future intentions of the Suba, fhe acquired fuch an empire over his mind, that he was brought to confent to the affaffination of Ayder, which fhe had projected in a manner that, in its own nature, was almoft certain of fuccefs.

During his ftay at Rana Biddeluru, Ayder had dwelt in the palace of the kings of Canara, and was of courfe to refide there on his return. From this palace to a famous pagoda, there was a fubterraneous communication, known to very few except the queen. The queen had refolved to undermine the palace, and to blow up Ayder the night of his return, when he fhould be at table with his principal officers,

officers *, hoping, that at the inftant of the cataftrophe, the people and foldiers of Canara, animated by her fon, might eafily put the troops of Ayder to the fword in their firft confufion and diforder.

This project might have been eafily put in practice by means of her hufband, the fuperior of the Bramins who belonged to the pagoda. The day of Ayder's return was come, and the moment approached in which this Suba and his retinue were to perifh by treachery ; when the plot firft came to the knowledge of a Bramin, chief of a pagoda fome leagues diftant from the city. Whether he was actuated, as the Bramins affirm, by a deteftation and horror for the crime ; or whether his hatred for the queen and her hufband, who were united contrary to their law, was his leading motive ; he conveyed himfelf in fecret to Rana Biddeluru, and, prefenting himfelf before Ayder, as if to compliment him on his happy return, he advifed him openly, in the prefence of the king and queen, of the confpiracy, and the danger he was in. This aftonifhing recital made the whole

---

* Ayder, like all the other Indians, makes two meals a day, the firft at eight in the morning, the fecond at midnight.

affembly tremble, but made no impreffion upon Ayder; who, looking round, difcovered the guilty perfons without difficulty. He ordered them to be feized. The witneffes were heard, and, the truth being eftablifhed on the fpot, the queen, her hufband, and all their accomplices, were put to death, except the king of Canara, who was carried prifoner to Maggheri, near Scirra, and his kingdom was confifcated.

The difcovery of this confpiracy was worth a fine kingdom to Ayder, rich in all forts of productions, and having a valuable extent of fea-coaft, with a good number of fea-ports. The immenfe quantities of rice, pepper, cinnamon, cardamoms, coral, fandal wood, and ivory, that abound in this kingdom, have caufed it to be called the granary and warehoufe of all India. In the mountains there are mines of gold, diamonds, rubies, and other precious ftones; and even in the very fortrefs of Rana Biddeluru, there is a rich gold mine. When Ayder took poffeffion of the place, he found an immenfe treafure in gold, coined and in ingots, in trinkets and precious ftones, that was indeed ftupendous, if credit may be given to the accounts of the French, who accompapanied him in that expedition. They fay that
the

the prince caufed pearls and precious ftones to be meafured in their fight with a corn meafure ; and that, having made two heaps of gold and trinkets, they furpaffed the height of a man on horfeback. On this happy occafion Ayder gratified all his troops with half a year's pay, not excepting thofe that were in garrifon in different parts of his dominions. He changed the name of Rana Biddeluru into that of Ayder Nagar, or Royal City of Ayder, and the name of Mangalor into that of Corial or Port Royal. He affumed at the fame time the title of King of Canara and of the Corgues, a fmall kingdom fituated at the fouthern extremity of Canara, and feparated from that kingdom, as well as from the Malabar diftrict, and the kingdom of Mayffour, by mountains that entirely enclofe it. It has long been in fubjection to the kings of Canara.

Ayder, after taking poffeffion of the capital, vifited the feveral parts of his new dominions, and was every where acknowledged fovereign with fcarce any oppofition. But being defirous of re-uniting certain cantons of this kingdom, in poffeffion of the Portuguefe, he did not find the viceroy of Goa difpofed to make this reftitution ; and, as he was far fuperior in force to the

I

the Portuguese, he did not hesitate to attack them.   With little difficulty he got possession of the country of Carvar and its fortress of Opir *, situated in the country of Sunda, formerly dismembered from the kingdom of Canara.   As he was preparing to lay siege to the fort of Rama, a fortress on the point of a cape of the same name, and the only barrier that could stop his progress to Goa, the French, who were under his command, refused to give him the least assistance, preferring rather to retire into the fort of Rama than to combat with the Portuguese : M. Hughel, siding with the French, abandoned him likewise.

Ayder, knowing it to be impossible to take this fort with his own troops, did not hesitate in making peace with the Portuguese, who yielded him the country of Carvar.   This inconstancy of the French, and other similar events, gave Ayder to understand that he should

---

* This fortress is much renowned for its strength. Ayder has augmented the fortifications.   The Portuguese and the Marattas have besieged it without success.   It defends the country of Carvar on the Portuguese side, and the entrance of the river Sangheri, that gives its name to a city at three leagues distance from its mouth, which is the capital of Carvar, and residence of a Catholic bishop.

not

not well fupport a war with any European power, and that he could not depend upon the Europeans in his fervice, excepting when they themfelves were at war with his enemies.

When Ayder came a fecond time to Man- galor, at his return from the war with the Por- tuguefe, he received a folemn deputation from a nation originally from Arabia, but now dif- perfed over the whole coaft of Malabar, and known by the name of Mapelets. At the head of this deputation was Ali, Raja or prince of Cananor. This Ali, fon of one of the moft rich and powerful Mapelets, had the good for- tune in his youth to be beloved by the daughter of the Raja of Cananor, a Nayre * prince.
The

---

* The Nayres are the nobility of the Malabar coaft. We may affirm that they are the oldeft nobility in the world ; for the ancient writers mention them, and quote the law that permits the Nayre ladies to have many hufbands ; every one being allowed four. Their houfes, which ftand fingle, have as many doors as the lady has hufbands. When one of them vifits her, he walks round the houfe, ftriking with his fabre on his buckler : he then opens his door, and leaves a do- meftic with his arms in a kind of porch, and who ferves to inform others that the lady is engaged. It is faid, that one day in the week the four doors are all open- ed, and all her hufbands vifit her, and dine together with her. Each hufband gives a fum of money, or portion,
at

The father, in fpite of the diverfity of religion, and the prejudice of his nation, which forbids all alliance with a different caft, and much more with ftrangers of another religion, confented to the marriage of his daughter with Ali, and dying, left him his principality, or the fmall kingdom of Cananor.

The Mapelets feem to be Arabs of Marcate and Sahar, who have fettled in India for the fake of commerce.   This nation, forming no alliance with ftrangers, has preferved its peculiar manners, and a particular phyfiognomy, much refembling that of the Arabs of Marcate, who have generally the face long, the chin fquare and turned up, and the beard thin.   They are lean, and of a fhort figure, not in the leaft refembling the other Arabs, who are large and handfome men, with black thick beards.

The inhabitants of the coaft of Malabar

at the time of marriage, and the wife only has the charge of the children.   The Nayres, even the Samorin, and the other princes, have no other heirs than the children of their fifters. This law was eftablifhed, that the Nayres, having no family, might be always ready to march againft the enemy.   When the nephews are of age to bear arms, they follow their uncles.   The name of father is unknown to a Nayre child. He fpeaks of the hufbands of his mother, and of his uncles, but never of his father.

having

having fuffered the Mapelets to take poffeffion of all the commerce of their country, as well by fea as by land, this nation has become rich and numerous, and that with ftill lefs diffculty, by reafon that the princes and nobles of the country, having frequent occafion for money, have often had recourfe to the Mapelets, who lent them large fums of money at exorbitant intereft; fometimes upon pawns, and fometimes in advance upon the harvefts of pepper, cardamoms, and rice. Thefe repeated * ufuries have increafed the riches of the Mapelets, and impoverifhed the princes or Nabobs of the Malabar coaft, known by the name of Nayres. The Mapelets grew proud in confequence of their wealth, and attracted the envy and jealoufy of the Nayres. Thefe laft, efpecially the more powerful of them, were not very exact in fulfilling their engagements

* Though the religion of Mahomet forbids ufury, the Mapelets make no fcruple in that refpect, notwithftanding they are great enthufiafts. The fhocking effects of their fanaticifm have been often feen at Mahé. In an excefs of zeal for their religion, the Mapelets intoxicate themfelves with opium, and devote themfelves to death for the fake of killing Chriftians and other enemies of their religion. They furioufly attack and kill all they meet, and do not ceafe till they are themfelves put to death.

with

with the Mapelets; who, on their part, were still more arrogant, when they saw Ali, a prince of their nation, elevated to the rank of prince of the country.

In this state of things, Ayder became master of the kingdom of Canara; and, consequently, a neighbour of the Malabar coast, of which the principality of Cananor is the frontier on the Canara side. Ali Raja, and the Mapelets, concluded that they should insure the possession of their states by putting themselves under the protection of Ayder, who was of the same religion, and whose power and reputation was capable either to protect or subjugate them.

The deputation of the Mapelets was honourably received by Ayder. He loaded their deputies with magnificent presents, and assured them of his protection and good-will. The Mapelets are navigators. Ali Raja had many vessels then well-equipped and ready to set sail. Ayder, who had resolved to have a fleet, in order to defend his coasts from the incursions of the Marattas and other pirates, created Ali Raja his high admiral, and made his brother, Sheic Ali, intendant of the marine, of the ports, and of the maritime commerce of his dominions.

dominions.—He intrufted him likewife with confiderable fums for the purpofes of purchaf-ing or of building veffels.

Ayder with juftice regarded his kingdom of Canara as the moft precious gift Providence had beftowed on him, and the beft inheritance he could leave to his children. He defigned Ayder Nagar to be the capital of all his do-minions. He caufed all his family to repair thither, except his firft wife, the fifter of Moctum, and mother of Tippou Saeb, his eldeft fon, who defired to refide at Bengue-lour. The intentions of Ayder were, to efta-blifh in this kingdom a government calculated to make himfelf beloved by his people; and he fucceeded beyond his hopes.—The govern-ment of his other ftates was fhared among his relations.

He left the government of Benguelour and its dependencies to Ibrahim Ali Khan, his un-cle, who had fo long enjoyed it. To Moc-tum Ali Khan * he gave the government of the kingdom of Mayffour; to Mirza, that

* In the patents given to his relations on this occa-fion, he prolonged their names. Thus, Moctum Saeb, or Mr. Moctum, was called Moctum Ali Khan, or Lord Moctum Ali.

VOL. I.   H   of

of Scirra, and all its diſtrict; and to a ſon of his uncle, named Amin Saeb, the government of the kingdom of Biſnagar.

Ali Raja having formed a ſmall fleet, at the commencement of the fair ſeaſon made the conqueſt of the Maldive iſlands, under the pretence of ſome injuſtice done to his nation; and after taking their king priſoner, he had the cruelty to put his eyes out. This conqueſt was made in the name, and on the account of Ayder, whoſe colours were borne by the fleet. Ali Raja had embarked on board a number of Seapoys, or diſciplined ſoldiers; ſo that Ayder's colours had no ſooner appeared at ſea, but they enforced reſpect.

Ali Raja having brought back his victorious fleet to Mangalor, came to Nagar to do homage to Ayder, and preſented to him the unfortunate king of the Maldives. Ayder, whoſe character is far from cruel, was ſo irritated at the barbarity of Ali Raja, that he inſtantly deprived him of the command of the fleet; which he afterwards gave to an Engliſhman named Stanet. Shocked at the inhumanity of Ali Raja, he entreated the king of the Maldives to forgive the outrage his admiral had been guilty of; and after expreſſing how much he was af-

flicted

flicted at the event, and ufing every argument in his power to confole him, he gave him one of his palaces for a retreat, with a revenue fufficient to procure all the pleafures his fituation permitted him to enjoy.

The courtiers and poets of this conqueror's court, little acquainted with geography, having learned that their mafter was become king of twelve thoufand iflands, added to his titles that of King of the Iflands of the Sea.

The conqueft of the kingdom of Canara, that had withftood the efforts of Aurengzeb; and that of the Maldive iflands, unknown to the greateft part of the Mogols, added fo much to the reputation of Ayder, that almoft all the princes of Indoftan difpatched ambaffadors to congratulate him on his numerous conquefts. The poets *, likewife, did not fail, in their poems, to fet him above Alexander and Timur.

It was now more than a year that Ayder had

---

* There are a great number of poets in Indoftan, efpecially in the courts, tho' Ayder does not value himfelf for the protection of poets and men of letters. There is a poet at court by appointment, who enjoys about £. 125 per month, or a thoufand rupees, and the rank of chief or general of a thoufand men : he compofes a poem on every event that adds to the reputation or glory of the prince.

not

not quitted the neighbourhood of Nagar, and that, occupied with the cares of government, and his pleafures, he appeared to be delighted with a ftate of repofe till then unknown to him.   At this juncture it was that the protection he had granted to the Mapelets recalled him to the head of his troops, and gave him an opportunity of making new conquefts.

The Mapelets, proud of the protection of Ayder, gave up that refpect and complaifance they had till then preferved for the Rajas and the other Nayres ; they even threatened to do themfelves juftice by force of arms, if the Nayres did not perform the engagements made with them.   The Nayres, whofe expences had compelled them to multiply the fums borrowed of the Mapelets, were fo befet by that nation of ufurers, that they were unable even to pay the intereft of the fums due, and faw nothing but ruin in the menaces of the latter.

Irritated as well by the arrogance as by the extortions of a race of people they were in the habit of defpifing, they refolved, at any rate, to diffolve the connection between them : for this purpofe feveral affemblies were held at Calicut, where the Zamorin, or chief of the Nayres refides, at which it was unanimoufly refolved, ed, that on an appointed day a general maſſacre of all the Mapelets ſhould be every where made. This conſpiracy was in part put in practice, and more than ſix thouſand Mapelets were murdered; though the greater number eſcaped. Their veſſels, ſpread over all the coaſt, favoured their eſcape; and in many places, being forewarned, they aſſembled in ſufficient numbers to reſiſt their enemies. The greater number took refuge at Cananor, where they found themſelves in ſecurity, by reaſon of its vicinity to the dominions of Ayder, as well as from the two ſmall fortreſſes of Cananor, one of which belonged to the Hollanders *, and the other to

Ali

* The Hollanders have ſince ſold their fort and territory to Ali Raja, which gave Ayder an opportunity of doing an act of juſtice to many hundreds of Chriſtians, inhabitants of Cananor, almoſt all of Portugueſe extraction. When the Dutch took Cananor from the Portugueſe they found a number of inhabitants round this fortreſs, whom they permitted to continue in the country. A great number of others have ſince come into Cananor, where they have built houſes, cleared the ground, and cultivated the gardens and fields. The Portugueſe and Dutch had granted the lands without any formality, and poſſeſſion was the only title of theſe poor people : when the Dutch ſold the fort and territory to Ali Raja, they made no ſtipulation in favour of the inhabitants. Ali Raja having demanded their titles, thought proper to force them to pur-

chaſe

Ali Raja. The Mapelets, in their diſtreſs, haſtened to ſend deputies to Ayder, to inform him of the cataſtrophe, and implore his protection. This nation, being fanatic Mahometans, their deputies repreſented to Ayder in their harangue, that God, and the prophet whoſe relation he was, had made him powerful for no other reaſon, than that he might protect the true believers; and that the crime of the infidels, which ought to be puniſhed by their deſtruction, would give him an opportunity of forming new conqueſts.

Ayder, who was already inſtructed in the power and force of the empire of the Nayres, and was acquainted with the difficulties that might oppoſe him in the conqueſt of the country, did not heſitate to promiſe juſtice and protection to the Mapelets. He quickly aſ-

chaſe the lands of which they ſuppoſed themſelves to be proprietors. This avarice of Ali Raja gave occaſion to the Engliſh to rail againſt the Dutch, of whom they had been deſirous of purchaſing the place. In their embarraſſment the poor inhabitants had recourſe to Ayder, who condemned Ali Raja upon the paſſage of the Alcoran, that ſays, " Thou ſhalt not take from the infidel his houſe, his field, &c. becauſe they were given him from God ; but thou ſhalt be content with cauſing him to pay tribute." Ayder fixed this tribute at a rupee, or nearly half a crown, a head.

ſembled

fembled twelve thoufand of his beft troops, of which four thoufand were cavalry, and the reft infantry, and began his march to the coaft of Malabar, directing his route by Mangalor and Cananor. All the artillery he took with him confifted of four pieces of cannon; and he ordered his fleet to accompany him along the coaft, to furnifh him with affiftance, as it might be required.

On his arrival at Cananor, he found more than twelve thoufand Mapelets under arms; ill armed, it muft be confeffed, but fuperior in courage to the Nayres, and animated by the defire of vengeance, and the hope of recovering their loffes at the expence of their enemies.

Ayder encamped on the banks of the river at Cananor, and difpatched an embaffy to Calicut, compofed of the moft diftinguifhed Bramins * of his court. They had orders to

reprefent

---

* The Bramins (who are the firft caft of Indians, deftined by their legiflature to be the priefts of their religion, as the Levites are by the law of Mofes) being become a very numerous body, have been forced to apply themfelves to other employs; and as they do not choofe to undertake any fervile employ, they are introduced into courts, where they do all kinds of bufi-

nefs,

represent to the Samorin, and all the Nayre princes, the injustice of the cruelties they had been guilty of to the Mapelets; and to inform them, that he was come with his army to see justice done them: but that, before he employed force, he judged it expedient to offer his mediation; promising, that if they would punish the principal offenders, and give a just and reasonable satisfaction to the Mapelets, his army should not advance into their country; and that he would even undertake the troublesome office of rendering justice to every one. The Nayre princes had agreed to support each other; and upon the report that Ayder was coming against them to the assistance of the Mapelets, they assembled an army of more than one hundred thousand men. The deputies of Ayder having finished their harangue, the Nayre princes replied, that they were astonished at the conduct of Ayder, with whom they had never had any connection or dependence; and that if his troops did any thing more than drink the

nefs, from the post of minister to that of spy: they are generally writers. Every lord, general, and even the lowest officers, have them in their service; a great number being forced to acquiesce in the pay of a private soldier.

water

water of the river of Cananor,—if they even
presumed to set their feet in the river, they
should be attacked and punished for their te-
merity. On this answer the ambassadors of
Ayder returned to their master ; and the
Nayres, having collected all their forces, appeared with the firm resolution to prevent
Ayder from passing the river.

The arrival of Ayder and his army on the
Malabar coast induced all the European nations who have establishments there to send
deputies to him.

Upon the great reputation of Ayder, it was
not doubted but he would make a conquest of
the whole country. The deputies of every
nation were in haste to treat with him for the
security of their factories and their commerce.
As they expected to find this great conqueror
at the head of a numerous army, they were
astonished to see so small a number of troops :
many of them could not help expressing their
surprise to the European officers of the army ;
magnifying, at the same time, the forces of
the Nayre princes, which they affirmed to exceed one hundred and twenty thousand men.
The officers answered, that since the Nabob, who
had it in his power to assemble a much greater

I army,

army, had brought no more than twelve thoufand men with him, it was to be prefumed,
that he was certain that the number he had
brought was fufficient to defeat his enemies.
This proper anfwer, which, to inſtructed and
enlightened men, would have had its due force,
made very little impreſſion on the deputies,
who had no notion of the military art, and
ſtill leſs of tactics : they made haſte to return
to their counting-houſes, well convinced that
the little army of Ayder would be deſtroyed
by that of the Nayres, who had lined the oppoſite bank of the river with a numerous artillery, and were continually firing and making
rhodomontades. Ayder, perfectly acquainted
with the genius of all the people of India, held
himſelf aſſured of the victory, and founded his
expectation on his cavalry; which was a body
of troops abſolutely unknown to the Nayres,
no foreign army having penetrated as far as the
Malabar coaſt, where no horſes had been ever
feen, except a few belonging to the European
chiefs of the factory, and purchaſed by them more
for pleaſure than utility : for this country, interfected by rivulets, and covered with woods,
befides being ſubject to continual rains for
feven months in the year, is abſolutely improper

proper for the breeding and keeping of horſes.

To ſucceed in his attempt, in ſpite of this numerous army and the artillery, Ayder cauſ-ed his fleet to enter the river. His veſſels ſailed up as far as poſſible ; and, drawing up his infantry in order of battle in a ſingle line in face of the enemy, with his twelve pieces of cannon, he waited for the ebb of the wa-ter. When the river was at the loweſt he entered it full gallop, at the head of his cavalry, which he had till then kept out of ſight of the Nayres : they were led on by fifty of the French huſſars, lately arrived from Pondicherry. As the rapidity of the current was diminiſhed by his veſſels, he traverſed the river without difficulty at a place where it was a league in breadth, ſometimes ſwimming, and ſometimes wading : he ſoon came to the other river, where the Nayres were buſied in attempting to oppoſe the infantry, who pre-tended to be on the point of paſſing over. They were frightened at the ſudden appear-ance of the cavalry, and fled with the utmoſt precipitation and diſorder, without making any other defence but that of diſcharging a

few

few cannon, which 'they were too much in-
timidated to point properly. Ayder, forefeeing
this event, had given orders to purfue the fugitives full fpeed, cutting down all they could
overtake, without lofing time, either by taking
prifoners, or fecuring plunder.

This order being executed with the utmoft
ftrictnefs, nothing was to be feen in the
roads, for the diftance of four leagues round,
but fcattered limbs and mutilated bodies. The
country of the Nayres was thrown into a general confternation, which was much increafed
by the cruelty of the Mapelets, who, following
the cavalry, maffacred all who had efcaped,
without fparing women or children : fo that
the army advancing under the conduct of this
enraged multitude, inftead of meeting with
refiftance, found the villages, fortrefies, temples, and in general every habitable place,
forfaken and deferted.   It was not till they
were near the environs of Tellicherry and
Mahé, French and Englifh eftablifhments,
that they began to find people, who had taken
refuge near thofe places.

Notwithftanding this general defection, the
army was in want of nothing : they every where
found

found cows, oxen, poultry, rice, and all forts of provifions that could be wifhed for in a fertile country ; the fugitives having abandoned every thing, without daring to load themfelves with the leaft article that could impede their flight.

Ayder caufed his army to halt near thefe fettlements, and fent an offer of peace to the Samorin, and other princes, on reafonable terms. The Samorin, who was old, remained quiet in his palace, and fent word, that he waited for the conqueror, and trufted to his difcretion.

This halt of the army, the fending of feveral Bramins, and more efpecially the tranquillity of the Samorin, encouraged the inhabitants, who returned for the moft part to their houfes : they were ftill more encouraged at finding that the Mapelets committed no outrages, except on the perfons or property of Nayres ; but the Nayres continued to conceal themfelves in the woods and mountains, from whence they carried on a kind of concealed war with the Mapelets.

Ayder marched for Calicut, and found no other refiftance in his route, but from a large pagoda, built on a mountain, and fortified.

In

In this place the nephew and presumptive heir of the Samorin had taken refuge, and found means to make his escape from thence, though it was invested: after his departure, the Bramins opened the gates to Ayder. The conqueror continued his journey to Calicut, and took up his residence at the English factory, where his fleet arrived before him. He enquired for the Samorin on his arrival, and was informed that he was in his palace, without any guard, waiting the commands of the conqueror; from whom he hoped for mild treatment, as he had always formally opposed the resolution to massacre the Mapelets, and had foretold the consequences to his nephews.

On this intelligence, Ayder returned into his * palanquin, and gave orders to advise the Samorin of his approaching visit. He met this prince, who came forth and threw himself at his feet ; Ayder hastened to raise him, and the Samorin offered his presents, consisting of two small basons of gold, one filled with precious stones, and the other with pieces of

* The palanquin is a kind of litter carried by six men. It is in common use in India, both for travelling and in cities, and is a very easy and convenient carriage.

gold,

gold, and two fmall cannons of gold, with carriages of the fame metal. The two princes having entered the palace, Ayder teftified the utmoft refpect for the Samorin, and promifed to reftore his dominions (on condition of his paying a fmall annual tribute) as foon as his fubjects had laid down their arms, and the affair of the Mapelets was amicably fettled. Thefe two princes parted, apparently much fatisfied with each other; but the world was highly aftonifhed, the next day, to behold the palace of the Samorin on fire; and though Ayder himfelf affifted in procuring help, it was impoffible to fave any thing, the edifice being entirely wood; and the Samorin, with all his family, and, as it is prefumed, much treafure, perifhed in the flames.

This prince had himfelf caufed the palace to be fet on fire, being refolved to terminate his life in that manner, on account of fome letters he had received from his nephews and the kings of Travancour and of Cochin *. Thefe letters contained the bittereft reproaches and execrations, treating him as the betrayer of his

---

* Thefe two kings were not tributary to the Samorin; but being of the fame caft as the Nayres, they made it a common caufe.

country,

country, and apoftate to his religion, which he had abandoned to the Mahometans. The Bramin who had conveyed thefe letters to him avowed to him at the fame time, that he was degraded and excluded from his caft ; and that all the Bramins and Nayres had fworn never to have any' communication with him. The tragical end of the Samorin affected Ayder extremely ; and he was fo irritated againft the nephews of that prince, that he publicly fwore he would never reftore their dominions.

The princes of Calicut, affifted by the kings of Travancour and Cochin, had collected a confiderable army on the river of Paniani, twelve leagues from Calicut, where they appeared difpofed to make better oppofition than they did near the river of Cananor. They had even collected together fome European cannoneers and Portuguefe artifans ; but upon the approach of Ayder, they had not the courage to face him, and faved themfelves by precipitately withdrawing their whole army. Ayder paffed the river, and attacked Paniani, which made very little refiftance, though the beft and almoft the only fortrefs in the country. He continued to purfue his enemies till he arrived at the environs of Cochin, where,

by

by the mediation of the Hollanders, he made peace with the king of that place, on his engaging to pay tribute.

The example of the king of Cochin was followed by the fubmiffion of all the Nayre princes; who fued for peace, and obtained it on condition of doing homage, paying tribute to Ayder, and rendering ample juftice each to the Mapelets in his refpective diftricts. On thefe terms they were all put into free poffeffion of their dominions; the nephews of the Samorin only being excluded from theirs.

After putting garrifons in Calicut and Paniani, Ayder beftowed the government of this ftate on the Raja of Coilmoutour, a Bramin, prince of a fmall country dependant on Mayffour, and feparated from the Nayres only by the mountains. He hoped that this prince, entitled to refpect from the Nayres, as being a Bramin, would be capable of maintaining peace and order, on account of his intimate knowledge of their manners and cuftoms.

The rainy feafon, which is very long and tempeftuous on the coaft of Malabar, began to appear, and obliged Ayder to quit the country:

VOL. I.   I   but

but in order to be at hand to watch his new conqueſt, he retired only to Coilmontour, the reſidence of the Raja, whoſe palace he occupied.

This country is beyond the mountains called *Gates*, and is not ſubject to the rains that overflow the coaſt of Malabar, from the middle of April to the end of September.

Paſſing by Madigheri, a large town and fortreſs on the frontier of the Malabar, at the diſtance of ſix leagues from Coilmoutour, Ayder left Raza Saeb, ſon of Chanda Saeb, in quarters, with three thouſand infantry.

Ayder imagined that the Nayres, awed by his power, and contented with his moderation, would peaceably ſupport the yoke he had placed upon them ; but he was not yet ſufficiently acquainted with the characters of that haughty people, who, once offended, never pardon their enemies, however great their wrongs.

The month of May was not yet elapſed, when a general revolt of the Nayres maniſeſted itſelf over all the coaſt of Malabar. It commenced by the maſſacre of a ſmall garriſon of about two hundred men, that were ſurpriſed by the inhabitants of a large town, called

Pondiaghari,

Pondiaghari, fituated at the foot of the fortrefs. They carried their cruelty fo far as to cut off five French foldiers, deferters from Mahé, who, intending to enter in the army of Ayder, arrived in the town the day after the maffacre: and, as a ftill greater inftance of the inhuman rage by which they were actuated, they ripped up two women who accompanied thefe unfortunate foldiers.

According to every appearance, this revolt was the effect of the fecret intrigues of the king of Travancour, and the nephews of the Samorin. It would doubtlefs have been lefs general, if the Raja of Coilmoutour, Ali Raja, and his brother Sheic Raja, who were intrufted with the charge of feeing the Mapelets reimburfed, had been more temperate in their rapines and exactions.

As the immenfe quantities of water that fall in the Malabar country convert the fmalleft rivulets into large rivers; and as this country offers an almoft infurmountable obftacle, by the torrents caufed by the overflowing of the waters, that are met with almoft at every ftep, during the rainy feafon; the Nayres, habituated to their climate, and going abfolutely naked in the ftormy months, believed, with reafon, that they fhould

I 2   have

have time to take Calicut and Paniani, and de-
ftroy the Mapelets, before Ayder could enter
their country ; but they were yet to learn,
that their conqueror was not to be ftopped
by obftacles much greater than thofe they depended on. They had taken their meafures
fo effectually, that Raza Saeb, commandant at
Madigheri, and Ayder, were ftill ignorant of
their revolt.

Calicut and Paniani were already invefted by
the army of the Nayres, when the news came
to Ayder, by means of a Portuguefe failor,
who, on the promifes of reward from the governor of Paniani, ventured to afcend the river
of the fame name alone, in a canoe made of
bamboo *, and covered with fkin. This failor, travelling only in the night, notwithftand-

---

* Thefe beats of bamboo, covered with fkin, are in fact
a kind of bafket ; and are of admirable ufe in armies,
more efpecially in the Malabar country. Ayder had a
great number in his army : two men carried the fkeleton
of one, and two more the fkin : in a quarter of an hour
they are ready for ufe ; and one boat will carry twenty-
five men, or a piece of cannon. The editor of the
Memoirs of General Lawrence makes fifty horfes enter
one of thefe boats ; but the fact is falfe : the horfe
fwims, and the horfeman, who is in the boat, holds the
bridle.

ing

ing the danger of wild beasts and noxious
reptiles, and with no other guide than a poc-
ket compass, arrived at Madigheri. He apprized Raza Saeb of the revolt, and the danger
to which Ayder's troops at Calicut and Paniani
were exposed.

This general, without loss of time, caused the
Portuguese to be conducted to Ayder at Coilmoutour; and himself immediately marched with
his forces towards Paniani, in spite of the rains,
and the inundation under which almost all the
country was laid by the overflowing of the rivers.
This precipitate march made some impression
on the revolters, as soon as they were apprized of it; but hearing that he had brought
no cavalry, they detached a party of their army, which harrassed Raza Saeb at the crossing
of each river, and at length succeeded (perhaps
by the fault of his guides) to draw him into
a place between the meeting of two rivers
that joined near Pondiaghari, where he found
himself shut up, without being able to pass
on either side, by reason of the depth and rapidity of the water; and cut off from returning by the defiles he had passed, which were
every where rendered difficult to pass, by fell-

I 3

ing

ing of trees, and the Nayres, who were in ambuſcade in various parts.

Ayder no ſooner heard of the revolt than he recalled a party of his cavalry that had been luckily cantoned near Coilmontour. While he was thus collecting the ſtrongeſt part of his army from Mayſſour and other parts of his dominions, he commanded a ſelect party of his infantry to be in readineſs to march on the ſhorteſt notice : however, in expectation that Raza Saeb might diſperſe the mutineers, he waited for news, before he expoſed to ſo inſalubrious a ſeaſon troops deſigned for very different operations.

Raza Saeb having contrived to ſend advice of his ſituation, Ayder immediately marched with three thouſand horſe, and ten thouſand Seapoys or Topaſſes. He ordered his cavalry, both officers and men, to ride without ſaddles; and commanded his infantry to quit their habits, and march naked, excepting a pair of light drawers and ſhoes. Each ſoldier was provided with a waxed cloth to wrap up his knapſack; and the three hundred Europeans lately arrived from Pondicherry and Colombo, were offered paraſols, as they did not chuſe to

quit

quit their habits. Their refufal was the caufe
that they were almoſt the only perfons in the
army that were attacked by the dyfentery.

All the artillery of this ſmall army confifted
in twelve light pieces of cannon, that were carried by elephants.

It is fcarcely poffible to form an idea of the
fpecies of war to which Ayder led his troops
this campaign. Imagine an army of fifteen
thoufand men marching from the break of day
through a mountainous country, in roads or
paffages fcarcely admitting more than three men
a-breaft, expofed from morning till night to a
conftant ſhower, equal to thofe that fall in the
greateſt ſtorms, attended with frequent thun-
der and lightning, excepting for three hours
after noon, in which the fun ſhone out with
almoſt infupportable luftre and heat ; frequent-
ly obliged to crofs rivers up to the chin in water, and fometimes fwiming ; and paffing the
night in towns or villages deferted by their inhabitants, where, however, they found plenty
of the neceffaries of life. Their path was every
where marked by ruin and deftruction, for
their orders were to burn and pillage, and they
exerted themfelves fo much in this horrible work;

that

that they left behind them nothing but heaps of ruins, where houfes had formerly ftood.

This unexpected march obliged the Nayres to collect all their troops, and gave fome relief to the troops of Raza Saeb, tho' not fufficient to prevent his lofing many of his men for want of neceffaries, and in confequence of the hard-fhips they were fubjected to.   The Nayre princes, tho' half defeated by the fear of the confequences of their revolt, neverthelefs ex-pected Ayder with confidence in a retrenched camp near Pondiaghari, which on its left wing had a village fortified with a ditch and parapet planted with pallifades, well furnifhed with ar-tillery, and maintained by the moft refolute, who had determined rather to perifh than yield. Ayder *, for the attack of this retrenched camp, difpofed of his army fo that four thoufand

---

* Ayder, before he made the attack, was perfuaded by his chief almoner, named Caka Saeb, to fuffer him to go near the Nayres, and perfuade them to furrender. This Perjada (for fo the doctors of their law are called) was fitting in a meadow with his brother, in conference with the deputies, when the enemy fired on him, and broke his brother's arm.   Some horfemen, whom his brother (then captain of artillery) had brought with him rode up, and helped them to efcape.

of his beſt Seapoys, forming the right wing, were charged to attack the village ; this corps was commanded by a Portugueſe lieutenant colonel *, lately arrived from Goa, with different officers of his nation. The left wing, compoſed of Topaſſes, was commanded by an Engliſh officer ; and Ayder himſelf commanded the main body, having behind him a reſerve of Europeans almoſt all French, with whom were joined thoſe who are called the *Bara Ademis*, or *Great Men*, a corps compoſed of all the young nobility and courtiers, without excepting even the generals, who have not appointed poſts or command on the day of battle. They were all on foot, and armed with ſabres and bucklers, having voluntarily put themſelves under the command of the officer of Europeans, whom

---

* Ayder being informed by Naza Saeb, who had reſided at Colombo for two years after the capture of Pondicherry, that all the European powers had introduced the Pruſſian exerciſe among their troops, wrote to Goa, Bombay, Pondicherry, Madras, Colombo, &c. to ſend him officers to diſcipline his troops. The Portugueſe lieutenant colonel had arrived from Goa on this occaſion. His improper manœuvre during the battle, and an unfortunate affair that happened to him the following night, cauſed Ayder to ſpeak harſhly to him; at which, being affronted, he demanded his diſmiſſion, and immediately obtained it.

they

they promifed to follow wherever he might lead them.

The cavalry, that could not be of fervice till after the entrenchment was forced, was formed behind the corps-de-referve. According to the orders, the Portuguefe officer attacked the re-trenched village with his four thoufand Sea-poys, by conducting them bravely to the edge of the ditch ; but, without advancing a ftep far-ther, he contented himfelf with caufing his troop to fire, as if at their exercife. Thefe un-fortunate Seapoys, totally expofed, were de-ftroyed with impunity by their enemies, who fired from pent-holes, or from behind the hedges. This firing, which lafted upwards of two hours, highly enraged Ayder, who receiv-ing every moment news of the ftate of the at-tack, learned with the utmoft mortification the unavailing lofs of his beft troops. The French officer, commandant of the Europeans, who lately arrived, and had not yet had an opportu-nity of diftinguifhing himfelf, offered to advance with the corps-de-referve, and put himfelf at the head of the Seapoys. Ayder anfwered, that he might do as he thought proper ; and he im-mediately joined his troop, which was impa-tient for the combat, and burned with a defire

to

to revenge the French who were inhumanly maffacred at Pondiaghari. Headed by this active and courageous officer, and joined by the Bara Ademis, they ran with violent eagernefs to the attack. The intervals between the battalions of Seapoys afforded them a paffage : they jumped into the ditch, and haftily afcending the retrenchments tore up the pallifades, and were in the face of the enemy in an inftant. They gave no quarter ; and the enemy, aftonifhed to the laft degree at their impetuofity and rage, fuffered themfelves to be butchered even without refiftance. The flames of the village on fire, and the direction of the cannon now pointed on the diftracted Nayres, evinced to Ayder that the village was carried. The whole army, in confequence, moved to attack the retrenchment ; but the enemy, perceiving that Ayder's troops had ftormed their out-poft, and catching the affright of the fugitives, fled from their camp with diforder and precipitation.

Ayder had fuppofed his enemies would have exhibited more firmnefs on this occafion. This brave and fortunate attack, which was much exalted by the young nobility that fhared the glory, gave him infinite pleafure. He created

the

the French commandant Bahader upon the
spot; and in the evening presented him with a
patent, appointing him general of ten thousand horse, which is the highest military post
among the Mogols; at the same time declaring him general in chief of his artillery. He
likewise gave a gratification of thirty rupees to
every soldier, and twice that sum to each of
the wounded; of which there was a great
number, though no more than one died.—As
the Nayres had no bayonets, the wounds were
only cuts with the sabre, little dangerous
where ready assistance is to be had. The Europeans inspired the Malabars with a new terror
by this exploit; and Ayder, to increase it,
spread a report that he expected many thousand men from Europe: he added, that they
were a cruel people, and devourers of human
flesh; and that his intention was, to deliver
all the coast to their outrages. The rage and
fury by which his small handful of French
were urged on to revenge their murdered countrymen, gave much force to the belief the
wretched inhabitants were disposed to afford
to his reports. Wherever he turned, he found no
opponent, nor even any human creature; every inhabited place was forsaken; and the poor
inhabitants,

inhabitants, who fled to the woods and mountains in the moſt inclement ſeaſon, had the anguiſh to behold their houſes in flames, their fruit-trees cut down, their cattle deſtroyed, and their temples burned *. The perfidy of the Nayres had been too great for them to truſt the offers of pardon made by Ayder, by means of Bramins he diſpatched into the woods and mountains to recall theſe unhappy people; who were hanged without mercy, and their wives and children reduced to ſlavery, whenever they were found in the woods by the troops of Ayder; ſeverity and mildneſs being both equally ineffectual in making them return to their homes.

* The Sieur Pocot de la Mothe, French commandant at Mahé, had written to the commandant of Europeans in the army of Ayder, to take the trouble, on this occaſion, to ſearch for the Vedam, and Ouzam Vedam, tranſcribed (if the fact be credible) before the time of Alexander; M. le Duc d'Ayen, now Marſhal Duc de Noailles, having given him a commiſſion to procure them at any price. The officer, deſirous of complying with the wiſh of this nobleman, cauſed different Bramins to look over the vaſt quantities of books, compoſed of plates of copper, held together by dozens by rings, which were deſtined by the captor to be caſt into cannon. The Bramins charged with this examination, who were no other than the writers or ſecretaries in the army, informed

him

homes. Ali Raja, and the Mapelets, who faw
themfelves thus involved in the ruin of the
Nayres, perfuaded Ayder to return to Coilmoutour, in hopes that his abfence might remove the timidity of the people : and it is
highly probable that the dyfentery that raged
in his army was a much more effectual reafon
that induced him to leave the country. The
officers and Europeans, who had retained their
clothing, and had more particularly abufed the
liberty of doing as they pleafed, were the moft
expofed to this dangerous malady.

. Before he quitted the country, Ayder, by a
folemn edict, declared the Nayres deprived of
all their privileges ; and ordained that their

him that all thefe books contained nothing more than
accounts of the expences of the pagodas, with the
names of the Bramins and their children. Some of
thefe books that were preferved, and afterwards put
into the hands of more learned Bramins, were found
to contain an enumeration of names of Bramins.
What makes it reafonable to fuppofe thefe books were
of little value, is their being written in *Tambou*, the
modern language of the Malabars ; and the ancient
language is the *Ouria* tongue, preferved by the priefts
of the Chriftians of St. Thomas, whofe religious rites
are performed in that language.—There is a printing-
office at Rome for books in this tongue, where the
Propaganda caufe miffals and breviaries to be printed
for their priefts.

caft,

caft, which was the firft after the Bramins, fhould thereafter be the loweft of all the cafts; fubjecting them to falute the Parias and others of the loweft cafts, by ranging themfelves before them, as the other Malabars had been obliged to do before the Nayres; permitting all the other cafts to bear arms, and forbidding them to the Nayres, who till then had enjoyed the fole right of carrying them; at the fame time allowing and commanding all perfons to kill fuch Nayres as were found bearing arms. By this rigorous edict Ayder expected to make all the other cafts enemies of the Nayres; and that they would rejoice in the occafion of revenging themfelves for the tyrannic oppreffion this nobility had till then exerted over them.

This ordinance being found to make the fubmiffion of the Nayres abfolutely impoffible, becaufe they would have thought death preferable to fuch a degradation, he made a new edict, by which he re-eftablifhed in all their rights and privileges fuch Nayres as fhould embrace the Mahometan religion. Many of thefe nobles took the turban on this occafion; but the greater part remained difperfed, and chofe rather to take refuge in the kingdom of Travancour than fubmit to this laft ordinance.

7

Though

Though the approach of the fine feafon, and the terror he had fpread, might have left little apprehenfion of another revolt, yet he left feveral bodies of troops in the country, diftributed in pofts fo fituated as to affift each other in cafe of neceffity, and quartered the reft of his infantry in the neighbourhood of Madigheri, taking only his cavalry with him to Coilmoutour, which he was obliged to fpread over the country, on account of the fcarcity of forage.

On his arrival at Coilmontour, Ayder found there a body of four thoufand Maratta cavalry lately arrived. More than a year had elapfed fince he had ordered this corps to be raifed, and fince the chiefs had received the neceffary fums of a Bramin, named Chamrao, formerly attached to Monf. Buffi, but fince entered into the fervice of Ayder, whofe confidence he had acquired. This Bramin had not been fufficiently fparing of the money; and when the Marattas had received it, they were in no hafte to complete their engagements. Inftead of three months, they were fcarcely ready to march in eight. Their horfes, inftead of being of the height and quality agreed on, were moftly fmall, fuch as are ufed by fervants,

vants, and called Tatoos in India. In fhort, inftead of a regular body of cavalry, it was nothing more than a collection of peafants and vagabonds, incapable of forming a line, or indeed of doing any thing, but rob and pillage. Secure in poffeffion of the Bramin's money, they paid little regard to his complaints; and, in order to avoid lofing the whole, he was obliged to take the troops, fuch as they were. When they were on their journey, they advanced very flowly, and made continual ftops; fo that inftead of one month, they employed four in making their journey; and even that degree of expedition was not obtained, but in confequence of repeated fums advanced by the diftreffed Chamrao.

The Marattas would not have acted in this manner, if they had been acquainted with the character of Ayder; who, for the fake of œconomy, was in the habit of requiring an exact account of the fums expended for the maintenance of his troops, and was not eafily deceived. In fact, having paffed them in review the day after his arrival, he found them in fo bad a ftate that he could not avoid expreffing his furprize to the Bramin. Chamrao had long fince written to Ayder, com-

VOL. I.   K   plaining

plaining of the mutiny and difobedience, not only of the private men, but of their officers. Ayder complained to the chiefs, that his orders were fo ill executed : he fignified to them, that, on account of their diforderly appearance and bad equipment, he would receive the troops, as his cuftom was with all his cavalry, and reform all thofe that were not agreeable to the agreements made with Chamrao, his agent: that he likewife expected they would account for all the money employed in raifing the troop ; and befides, to fhew them his difpleafure to find, that, regardlefs of every thing that could be urged by the perfon intrufted with his orders, they had employed in their journey four times the fpace neceffary to perform it in, he had given orders to his treafurer to deduct from their account the time they had voluntarily loft by paffing through unufual roads.

Thefe Marattas, who, according to their own account, had large fums to receive, murmured loudly at finding themfelves obliged to renounce a confiderable part of their claim. Not at all habituated, in their own country, to be commanded defpotically, they refolved with one accord to return to their camp ; with

I

menaces

menaces to do themfelves juftice, if refufed it by fair means.

They who knew Ayder, and how circum-fpect he is, could not conceive how he could fo indifcreetly put himfelf in the power of thefe Marattas; having kept with him at Coilmou-tour no more than five hundred Seapoys, and thirty Europeans, who were their comman-dant's guard.

Fortunately, the Maratta troops were not ignorant that Ayder was able, in a very fhort time, to collect military of every denomina-tion: in the mean time they demanded pay-ment within the hour, or in default they threatened to mount their horfes, and return into their own country, deftroying and pillaging all that might offer in their way.

Ayder reproached himfelf fecretly for the vivacity that had led him to ufe menaces with thofe people, at an inftant in which he was not prepared to give law to them. Though he had little to fear perfonally, it would have been more prudent in him to have retired at this juncture into the fortrefs of Coilmoutour; but that courage, which never abandoned him, led him to furmount the difficulty and danger that now prefented itfelf.

In

In this embarraſſment Maſſous Khan, ancient Nabob of Arcot, and brother of Mehemet Ali, adviſed him to ſend for the French
commandant, and give him the charge of re-
ducing this mutinous cavalry to reaſon. Ayder approved of the thought, and ſent for the
officer : he explained the affair to him, and
informed him that, by the advice of the Nabob of Arcot, he requeſted he would undertake to bring thoſe vagabonds to hear reaſon ;
whom he could eaſily reduce by force of arms,
but that he wiſhed to uſe milder methods.
The French officer conſented to ſhew himſelf
worthy of the confidence Ayder honoured him
with, though he ſaw all the difficulty attending the execution of the buſineſs : however,
he undertook it with ardour, being deſirous of
continually rendering himſelf more uſeful and
neceſſary.

To begin his negociation, he ſent word to
the Maratta chief, that he was deſirous of
paying him a viſit, in order to cultivate an
acquaintance with him and the other great
men of his nation : at the ſame inſtant he
ſent an expreſs for Madigheri, with orders for
all the Europeans to march for Coilmoutour ;
and, together with his letter, he diſpatched an

7

order

order from Ayder to the commander in chief of the cantonment, to fend off all the Topaffes, which amounted to a body of above four thoufand men.

The Maratta chief having accepted with joy the vifit the French officer propofed, received him with the greateft politenefs, as did the other chiefs who were affembled on the occafion. In order to obtain their confidence, the commandant, after making the ufual compliments (that is to fay, fpoken highly of the valour and merit of the Maratta nation) proceeded to inform them, that he wifhed to vifit them, becaufe the French and himfelf were nearly in the fame fituation as the Maratta cavalry; and it might be found advantageous to unite their pretenfions, and make a common caufe. The fact in reality was, that the French troops arrived in Ayder's dominions at the very juncture in which the revolt of the Nayres demanded his attention, and had remained a confiderable time at Syringpatnam. It is true, that he had received confiderable fums by order of Ayder; but, though he had already been engaged in actual fervice, no agreement had yet been made for the emoluments and pay of himfelf and his troops.

K 3 This

This overture having infured the confidence of the Marattas, they began to exclaim againſt Ayder, and accuſed him of breach of faith, by ſpeaking almoſt all at once; their chief at laſt found an opportunity of ſpeaking alone: he ſpoke highly of the conduct and behaviour of his troops, and placed their pretenſions in the moſt favourable point of view; and the French officer, ſeeming to give credit to their words, was careful not to ſhew any intimation that he was charged with any commiſſion from Ayder: he gave them reaſon to ſuppoſe the contrary; and even acquainted them (as in confidence) that he expected his troop the next day, who, impatient to know their fate, would come expreſsly to decide it : that therefore he judged it expedient for them to wait till the Europeans were arrived; and in the mean time, he would go to Ayder, as if from himſelf, and offer his mediation : the Marattas unanimouſly approved this project, and accepted his offer with gladneſs. Things thus adjuſted for the preſent, there was no queſtion concerning the expediting of buſineſs : the Marattas promiſed the French officer, that they would return his viſit the following day at the ſame hour, to learn the effect of his

intended

intended conference with Ayder; and they parted good friends. All the country refounded with the valour of the French; and the Marattas, who had the higheft opinion of them, on account of the defeat of Nazerzing, and the exploits of M. Buffi *, were highly flattered with this kind of alliance with them.

The following day the few Europeans that were at Madigheri, to the number of four hundred men, began to appear, but irregularly, in fmall numbers, confifting of three or four at moft in a party. By this artifice, they appeared to be coming in all day, without its being poffible for the Marattas to judge of their number; and thofe who arrived did not fail to acquaint the enquirers, that the main body would foon arrive: accordingly, at the clofe of the night, a column of infantry paffed by the Maratta camp, with

---

* This ought not to be taken for flattery. The Author has long ago affured the people in power, that M. Buffi enjoys the higheft reputation in Indoftan; and it is certain, that a Frenchman among the Marattas, or in the army of the Suba of Decan, will be every moment afked *Mouffa Buffi qu'an é?* or, what is become of M. Buffi?

K 4   drums

drums beating and colours flying, compofed of Topaffes *, who had been fent from Madigheri, and were headed by the Europeans who, by another route, had went out of Coilmoutour to join them.

This artifice caufed the Marattas to believe the Europeans were much more numerous than they really were ; and their notion was ftrengthened by the hats of the Topaffes, and their drums and fifes, which refemble the

---

* The Topaffes are black Chriftians, who call themfelves Portuguefe, and have the names of the firft families in Portugal ; but who, to all appearance, are defcended from flaves, born and brought up in the houfes of the Portuguefe, who treat very favourably, and with great humanity, thofe flaves whom they call Creanza de Caza, or Children of the Houfe. The Europeans have never been able to form good troops out of thofe people ; which arifes, no doubt, from the contemptuous manner they treat them with : inftead of which, Ayder has always put them on an equality with the Seapoys, and even preferred them to his other troops; as will be feen in the courfe of this Hiftory. The officers of thefe Topaffes are Europeans ; which circumftance, however, does not prevent thofe among them who diftinguifh themfelves, from being promoted : in confequence of this treatment, they may be regarded as Ayder's beft troops, and thofe he can moft rely on.

others ;

others ; and as they played the fame marches, and it was almoft dark when they appeared, it was not eafy to perceive the difference.

The principal Maratta chiefs waited on the French commandant; who receiving them with the moft attentive politenefs and regard, acquainted them, that he had found Ayder difpofed to act in the moft amicable manner with them, and had accepted his mediation ; but that he had promifed to keep ftrictly to the agreement made with his agent, Chamrao : that he confented, either that himfelf alone, or with fuch other perfons of confequence as the Marattas might chufe, would pafs in review, one by one, the horfemen and their horfes, for the purpofe of reforming thofe that were not according to the agreement : and likewife, that after having taken an account of the length of the journey they had had to perform, arbitrators fhould decide the time they ought to have employed. The French commandant added, that thefe propofitions having appeared to him equitable, he had judged it proper to fubmit, and accept them; being well convinced of the candid and noble manner of thinking that diftinguifhed the Maratta nation.

They,

They, who did not find their account in this method of adjufting the affair, exclaimed much againft the facility of the officer, and affured him that they would not confent to be thus paffed in review ; and more particularly becaufe Chamrao, the envoy of Ayder, had feen and approved the horfes, which had not fince been changed ; and that with refpect to his demand concerning the time employed in the journey, it was at the very requeft of Chamrao, they affirmed, that they had fojourned on the road, in order that they might not arrive at Coilmoutour during the abfence of the Nabob, being informed that forages were very rare.   Thefe Maratta officers having perfifted in their determination, maintained firmly that the propofitions made to them were unreafonable ; and that they could not accept them, nor abate their pretenfions, without the confent of all the chiefs, of whom they would convene an affembly.   The night approaching, they returned very diffatisfied with their vifit, and the refolution of Ayder.

The French officer, not to render himfelf fufpected by paying too great attention to the fituation of their encampment, thought proper to commit that charge to one of his adjutants,

tants *. This officer reported that the camp was in a meadow fituated between two banks, one ferving to retain the water of a great tank, and the other as a paffage at the time of rain ; that the meadow was bounded at one end by a hill impracticable to cavalry, becaufe covered with fruit-trees, and interfected by hedges and walls of earth, that divide the property of different perfons ; that at the extremity of the bank, that ferved for a road, there were fome houfes, and a fmall pagoda ; and, laftly, that he was of opinion, that two hundred men, and fome pieces of cannon, placed in this hamlet, would be able to prevent the Marattas from going out of their camp. In confequence of this advice, cannon were conveyed in the night to this poft, and 250 men, who entrenched themfelves. A barbette battery of ten pieces of cannon was conftructed, which was by no means an agreeable fight to the Marattas when day-light appeared. Their chiefs having fent to the officer who commanded the poft, to demand with what intention thofe cannon were pointed at their camp, received anfwer, that they had been

---

* This adjutant was M. de Lallie, who now commands a corps in Ayder's army of two hundred and fifty European horfemen ; of which he is proprietor, as well as of a regiment of Seapoys.

placed

placed there by his commandant, with orders
to fire on the firft Maratta that fhould attempt
to get on horfeback ; and that if they defired
farther information, they muft apply to the commandant. On this they difpatched two of
their officers, who complained of this act of
hoftility, but with much politenefs, and an air
that fufficiently exhibited their fear. The commandant did not hefitate to anfwer, that having
been fo little fatisfied the preceding evening
with their reception of the propofitions of Ayder, which to him appeared juft and reafonable ;
and fearing that, by a precipitate refolution of
returning into their own country, they might
betray his faith and honour, pledged to the fovereign on their account, he thought it incumbent on him to take thefe precautions. But,
neverthelefs, he wifhed to continue his mediation, and would certainly join them, if Ayder
refufed to do them juftice. This difcourfe having encouraged them, they protefted they were
ready to treat ; and that, trufting entirely to his
promifes, all the chiefs would wait on him at an
hour to be appointed, for a conference with Ayder's minifters.

On the affurance given them that no act of
hoftility fhould be committed, provided they
remained

remained quiet in their camp, they returned to their quarters. The commandant repaired to Ayder to inform him of their good difpofitions: he found him alone with Maffous Khan, who likewife offered himfelf as mediator and inter-preter, for which he was qualified by fpeaking very good Portuguefe.

In confideration of the advanced age and high rank of this perfonage, the French officer begged he would confent that the meeting might be held at his houfe. Advice was given to the Marattas, who repaired thither at the clofe of the evening. Two Bramins, fecre-taries to Ayder, likewife attended, and every thing was arranged in two days; Maffous Khan having removed all the difficulties with a degree of addrefs and intelligence very uncom-mon, but acquired by fifty years experience in this fort of negociations. It was agreed, that none fhould be difmiffed but fuch horfes as were abfolutely incapable of any kind of fervice; that they fhould all pafs in exact review; that fuch as fhould be judged in a ftate to ferve as good cavalry, fhould be paid at the rate of forty ru-pees a month, man and horfe, according to the agreement made with Chamrao; and that the others fhould be reduced to five-and-twen-

ty,

ty, and fhould ferve as irregular cavalry. The time allowed for the journey was fet at three months.

After this review it was found that one hundred and fifty horfe only were entitled to forty rupees, and the reft were reduced to five-and-twenty. The principal chief, whofe troop was well mounted, and who alone poffeffed eight hundred horfe, had none difmiffed ; perhaps there was indulgence fhewn him, on account of the pains he had taken to accommodate the difference.

The affair being thus fatisfactorily adjufted, Ayder made a prefent of twenty-two horfes to the French officer, to mount twenty Europeans, to ferve him as a guard, and accompany him every where : at the fame time he gave orders to the Bacfi * and the fecretary at war, to fettle the pay and emoluments of all the Europeans ; Ayder being in the cuftom never to fettle his pecuniary affairs himfelf, but committing the charge of them to minifters, who have no permiffion to conclude any bufinefs without the precife orders of their

* The Bacfi is properly the minifter at war, and the fecretary is fubjected to his orders, though generally he is the confidential minifter of the Nabob.

mafter.

mafter. To make their court, the Bacfi and his
colleague exclaimed againft the exorbitant pretenfions of the Europeans, and propofed abatements that were flatly rejected : but as the
corps of Europeans was not numerous, the
fubject of thefe difcuffions was of fmall confequence to Ayder : to end them therefore,
and to make a parade of generofity that he
thought fuitable to his rank, he ordered the
commandant and principal officers before him,
and, addreffing himfelf to the former, " I hear,
with concern," faid he, " that you do not agree
with the Bacfi and Narimrao. Why did not you
apply to me ? have you forgot that I have, both
by writing and converfation, informed you,
that you may difpofe of every thing I poffefs ;
and that the French are efteemed by me as
brothers ?" Upon which he gave orders to
Narimrao to prepare the Batis *, and he figned
them

* The Batis are fmall writings or warrants. Every
perfon in the military fervice has one, from the general to the drummer. This writing contains the name
of the perfon, and of his father and grandfather; a
defcription of his perfon, and that of his horfe (if he be
a horfeman) ; the day he entered the fervice; his ftation,
and his pay ; and as often as he is paid the fum is
entered on the fame : thofe of the officers contain
fimply the name, the ftation or degree, and the fums
received.

them before he difmiffed the officers; at the fame time inviting them to an entertainment to be given at the palace the next day.

As it could not be expected that the coaft of Malabar would ever enjoy a ftate of tranquillity while the Nayre princes were on the frontiers, and in the country of Travancour, Ayder refolved to make the conqueft of that kingdom; for which, however, he could urge no better reafon than that the king of that country had affifted his enemies. Though this kingdom is of fmall extent, it is very populous; and its king, Ram Raja, has acquired a reputation for his valour and prudence, which gave reafon to conclude that the undertaking would be attended with much difficulty.

Ayder knew that his enemy had long exerted himfelf in difciplining his army; that he had a numerous corps of Seapoys well

received. The Batis are triple, and in three different languages, Perfian, Maratta, and Canarin; and as there are three chancellors, they are preferved in the greateft order. Ayder figns the ftate of accounts every month, as well as a particular ftate for every troop; for no payment is made without the fignature of Ayder, or, in his abfence, of the general commandant.

armed,

armed, and a train of artillery ferved by good cannoneers, procured from the Danes, the Eng-lifh, and the Dutch. He likewife knew that the country was not to be penetrated but by way of narrow paffages through mountains, where Ram Raja had caufed fortreffes to be con-ftructed, which he was firmly refolved to defend to the utmoft. Neither was he' ignorant, that the Englifh, jealous of his power, had affem-bled troops in Madura and Marava, countries dependant on Mehemet Ali Khan, and fron-tier to Travancour : but, habituated to over-come all obftacles, he was determined to pur-fue his intention. He trufted to the promifes made by the Englifh deputies, who had waited upon him on the coaft of Malabar ; to whom he had granted not only a confirmation of all their former privileges, but had, befides, given permiffion to eftablifh a factory at Onor ; and he was likewife perfuaded, that the Englifh troops were affembled for no other purpofe than to protect the dominions of Mehemet Ali from infult.

Maffous Khan had lately been induced to take the part of Nizam Ali Khan, who had fent him prefents of great value. He knew that the Suba of Decan was engaged in wars with his vaſſals, in which he was aſſiſted by a party of Engliſh, commanded by General Smith. He therefore concluded that he had nothing to fear on his part.

In order to ſecure himſelf from any interruption in the war he had projected, Ayder wrote to Mirza Ali Khan, governor of Scirra, and his brother-in-law, to renew the truce with the Marattas, which was on the point of expiring: a buſineſs not difficult to be performed, by means of a ſum of money properly diſtributed among the chiefs.

The intended war, and the neceſſity of placing ſtrong garriſons in the conquered country, obliged Ayder to make conſiderable levies for the augmentation of his army; and, being willing to derive every advantage from the time preceding that in which he intended to march againſt Ram Raja, he cauſed all his troops and his artillery to be exerciſed by the European officers, he himſelf aſſiſting every day with his ſons and generals at the different exerciſes and evolutions.

After conſulting the commandant of Europeans, whoſe knowledge and intelligence he greatly valued and depended on, he eſtabliſhed, by his advice, a corps of five thouſand grenadiers,

nadiers, divided into battalions of five hundred men, compofed of four companies of one hundred and twenty-five men each. Two of thefe battalions were felected out of the Topaffes, and the reft from the Seapoys; each being commanded by an European officer. There was, befides, in each company, an European adjutant or ferjeant-major. The officers and private men of every company were chofen by Ayder himfelf, who regarded tallnefs lefs than a martial air, and the activity and robuft temperament of the individual.

Thefe grenadiers received ten rupees a month, inftead of eight, which is the pay of the other Seapoys. They were exempt from all works of labour, and even mounted no guard, except that of their commandant; and, that nothing might prevent their being ready to march at the firft fignal, every efcouade, compofed of feven men, including an inferior officer, were allowed a cook fervant, and an ox to carry their tent and baggage. Every company was augmented by an efcouade of feven men, deftined folely to guard the baggage. Thefe were as it were apprentices, being youths of about fixteen or feventeen years old, intended to replace the grenadiers who fell,

L 2

and

and to render the corps capable of affording great advantages by the rapidity of their motions. From the time of their firſt eſtabliſhment, they were exerciſed every morning in handling their arms, by their own officers; and every afternoon, from three till ſix, five battalions, by turns, were exerciſed in their evolutions by the French commandant; after which they were made to march from ſix to eight, marching out at the ordinary pace, and returning home with a quick ſtep.

All the officers, without exception, were obliged to do this exerciſe as well as the common ſoldiers. This conſtraint at firſt occaſioned much murmuring among them, but luckily it did not come to the hearing of Ayder. However, whether through a ſenſe of duty, or from example, they became accuſtomed to it, and their aſſiduity afforded great encouragement to the ſoldiers. It was thus that this ſovereign formed a body of troops, to whoſe rapid movements the Engliſh afterwards attributed all his ſucceſs.

The Engliſh had no ſooner heard of Ayder's preparations, which fame had rendered ſtill more conſiderable, than they conceived umbrage at them, as well as at the long ſtay he
                                        made

made at Coilmoutour, the capital of a fmall diftrict or country adjoining to Madura, of which we have already made mention. In their uncertainty refpecting his intentions, they refolved to difpatch his Ouaquil from Madras, a Bramin, named Menagi Bandec, to carry him a letter from the governor and council of that fettlement. This letter announced a folemn embaffy, compofed of Colonel Call, chief engineer, and Counfellor Bofchier, brother to the governor. Ayder being perfuaded that they intended to make propofitions to him, relative to Travancour and the coaft of Malabar, contrary to his views and intentions, thought it neceffary to elude the receiving the embaffy. He immediately difpatched an anfwer to the letter of the council, affuring them that he was very much flattered with their letter, and thanking them for the honour they intended him in fending fo diftinguifhed an embaffy ; but at the fame time he added, that Coilmoutour, being only a camp or military ftation, by no means proper for the reception of ambaffadors with thofe honours they were entitled to expect, he could not decently receive the embaffy till he fhould arrive at Syringpatnam, a royal city, to which he propofed to return

L 3

in a short time; and that he would be careful to advise the governor of Madras of his arrival there.

Ayder was too well acquainted with the English politics to suffer himself to be seduced by the pompous honour with which they hoped to dazzle his sight; and, far from being flattered with this embassy, he was determined no longer to defer his expedition against Travancour. The order was already given for the army to be in readiness to march, when an unforeseen event convinced him that he had more enemies than he suspected, who were anxiously intent upon his destruction.

There was an Irish officer in his army, named Turner, who had been admitted into his service by virtue of a letter of recommendation from Governor Boschier. He was a man of a strong understanding; and who, possessing all the talents required in a good soldier, especially in the art of tactics, had in a very short time gained the affection of Ayder, who committed the most important operations to his care. This man, who was not in the slightest degree suspected, was commander of the first battalion of Topass grenadiers; and, in this quality, he was regarded as general of that military,

litary, which forms a body of about five thoufand men.

It muſt be allowed that an officer recommended by an Engliſh governor ought to have
been treated with lefs confidence and fecurity ;
but this man had behaved fo well in the war
on the coaſt of Malabar, that, far from having
any miſtruſt of him, he had acquired the confidence of his generals. Taking advantage of
the good opinion they had of him, he waited
till the time of payment, which is made the
fifth day of every lunar month after the moon
has appeared ; and when he had received his
appointments, and the pay of his men, he made
his efcape by the road that leads towards Cochin.

His quarters were a fhort league diftant from
Coilmoutour. The officers of his corps waited on him to receive their pay ; but, under the
captious pretence of his fecretary being abfent,
he begged them to wait till the next day, which
was without difficulty granted. To put his
project in execution he mounted his horfe, being accompanied by a young Swediſh officer,
to whom he had communicated his defign, and
difappeared, carrying every thing of value he
poffeffed with him ; taking the precaution firſt

to

to acquaint his domeftics that he was going to fupper with the commandant-general at Coilmoutour.

The intenfity of the heat in the day, and the beauty of the nights, in India, induce people of diftinction to fit up very late, more efpecially as they have the cuftom of fleeping in the day from three till fix. Some officers, who were in this habitude, called upon him, and were aftonifhed to find he was gone to fupper at Coilmoutour; but far from harbouring any fufpicion, they concluded, on the contrary, that it was a gaming party, knowing him to be a great gamefter. The night being fine, they refolved to take the advantage of it; and, thinking to furprife him agreeably, they mounted their horfes, and repaired to the commandant's quarters at Coilmoutour, where they arrived about midnight. Their aftonifhment was highly increafed, when they found every body in the moft profound fleep. They enquired to no purpofe for Turner, as no one could give any account of him; and the fufpicion that confequently arofe in their minds induced them to apply to the commandant himfelf. On their account of the abfence of their officer, the commandant fent to enquire of the pofts that

2   guarded

guarded the entrance of the paffes, whether any one had paffed them ; and was informed, that two European officers had departed three hours before. The firft captain of Turner's corps, named Minerva, an Irifhman, offered to purfue him inftantly with a party of fifty Europeans : his offer was accepted, and he departed at two in the morning. At eight they had ftretched over upwards of fix leagues, and arrived at the frontier of the country of Cochin. They difcovered the horfes of the officers they were in queft of, and environed the houfe, in which they found them both afleep. They immediately fecured their perfons, and conducted them bound to Coilmoutour.

Ayder being informed of the efcape of Turner and the Swedifh officer, and of their recapture, gave orders to judge them as in a fimilar cafe in Europe. In confequence, a court martial was affembled, at which the two criminals were tried, and convicted of carrying off the public money : fentence was accordingly pronounced, that they fhould be degraded and hung, and their bodies afterwards expofed on the high road. The council, in compaffion to the

the youth of the Swedifh officer (who, according to all appearance, had been feduced
by the other, and ftill more, becaufe he carried away no property of any other, and was
only culpable in having departed without leave)
thought proper to intercede with the Nabob
in his favour ; who commuted the punifhment
of death into that of imprifonment. As to
Turner, he was conducted to the place of punifhment, and there difcovered to the council,
that the Englifh, conjointly with Nizam Ali
Khan, intended to attack Ayder. He confeffed
that he was a fpy employed by the government
of Madras, and begged pardon of the fovereign
for having fo long abufed his confidence ; that
he fhould not have made his efcape, if he had
not lately been nominated major of a regiment
on the Bombay eftablifhment : he intreated his
judges, in confideration of the importance of
his difcoveries, they would fpare him the indig-
nity of being hanged, and, as he deferved to die,
would give orders for him to be fhot : this requeft was allowed him. Before he fuffered, he
diftributed all his money to the foldiers appointed to put him to death ; to the Sieur Minerva he gave his fword and watch. After
his

his death he was fufpended on a tree near the road-fide, conformably to the latter part of his fentence.

The difcovery of the intentions of the Englifh, caufed the departure of the army for Travancour to be fufpended. Ayder without delay caufed Maffous Khan to repair to Ayder Abad, where he was charged to attempt, by the intrigues of his friends and his creatures about the Nabob, who were in great number (Bazaletzing, brother of the Subah, being the firft) to avert the ftorm that threatened him from that court.

In the mean time he continued to exercife his troops, and train them to all kinds of evolutions. This fpectacle, entirely new to the Indians, and the long ftay of the fovereign of fo many ftates in Coilmoutour, drew fo great a concourfe of people to that place, that their number amounted to more than 100,000, exclufive of the army, which exceeded 60,000 : but it will fcarcely be credited, that this country is fo abundant with all the neceffaries of life, that a fheep or a dozen of fowls never coft more than two fhillings ; and twelve meafures of rice, one of which is fufficient to ferve a man a day, were fold at the fame price. The
immenfe

immenſe population of this country is proved
by the two markets which are held weekly ;
where, at each, is commonly ſold twenty thouſand pieces of ſilk, each fourteen cubits long *.
This country, through which lies the ordinary paſſage from Mayſſour and the coaſt of
Coromandel, to the coaſt of Malabar, pro-
duces a conſiderable revenue to Ayder, who
enjoys the tolls, to the excluſion of the Rajas
of the country.

It is eſtimated, that thirty thouſand oxen,
loaded with tobacco, annually paſs through
Coilmoutour : this aſſertion is rendered very
probable, by the numerous magazines of that
commodity at Pondiagheri. Beſides tobacco,
there are great quantities of ſilks of every kind,
and pepper, cardamom, ivory, &c. brought
from the coaſt of Malabar.

During the long ſtay of Ayder at Coilmoutour, many events happened, which, though
of no great importance, are yet ſufficiently in-
tereſting to be related. They may ſerve
not only to give the reader a more perfect

---

* The ſuperior of the Jeſuit miſſionaries, who re-
ſides at Xavier Paleam, one mile diſtant from Coilmoutour, has aſſured me, that he had ten thouſand Chriſtian weavers in his miſſion.

idea

idea of the genius and character of Ayder, but likewife to throw light on the manners of the people, of whom the Nabob is become the fovereign. The firft of thefe events is a procefs or fuit at law, carried on againft the miffionary Jefuits of the dominions of Ayder.

The news of the expulfion of the felf-named Jefuits from Portugal and France having arrived in India, a miffionary of that order, a Portuguefe by nation, and refiding in Mayffour, quitted his cure in 1767, and retired to Goa ; being determined, as he faid, to fhew himfelf a faithful fubject of his king, by no longer continuing in a body of men declared to be enemies of his country. A year and a half after his departure, he wrote to a Portuguefe lady, named Madam Mequinez, widow of a Portuguefe officer, who had rendered fignal fervices to Ayder, and was afterwards flain in a battle againft the Marattas: Ayder, in return, had given his widow the regiment of Topaffes her hufband had poffeffed, with the appointment of colonel, till an adopted fon of her hufband's was of age to command the regiment himfelf.

This lady accompanied her regiment every where : the colours were carried to her houfe ;

houfe; and fhe had a private fentinel at the door. She received the pay, and caufed the deductions to be made in her prefence from each company. When the regiment was collected, fhe infpected them herfelf, as well as all the detachments that were ordered out; but fhe permitted the fecond in command to exercife the troops, and lead them againft the enemy.

This dame Mequinez having received the letter of the ex-jefuit father, addreffed herfelf to the Bramin Narimrao, fecretary at war, and much efteemed by Ayder. She complained that, during the life, and fince the death of her hufband, fhe had depofited in truft in the hands of the now ex-jefuit, all her jewels, and the money fhe and her hufband could fpare: that this father having departed to Goa, fhe, being in the army, wrote to him, and received for anfwer, that all the jewels and money fhe had depofited in his hand, were transferred, under the fame title, into thofe of the provincial father refident at Xavier Paleam, to whom it was neceffary for her to addrefs herfelf for reftitution: fhe added, that having carried this letter to the provincial father, he affirmed, fhe had loft her fenfes;

fenfes ; and that he had never heard either of her money or her jewels : at the fame time fhe placed in the hands of the fecretary the letter received by her from Goa, together with a ftate of the jewels and money fhe reclaimed, amounting to a confiderable fum. The Bramin acquainted Ayder with the particulars of this affair, and painted the Jefuits in the moft odious colours, by reciting what had paffed in France and Portugal concerning them.

On this complaint, Ayder immediately ordered a guard of four Seapoys and a corporal to every miffionary found in his dominions, with orders not to lofe fight of the reverend fathers ; but at the fame time to permit them to perform their functions, as well in their miffions as in their churches, without impeding them in the leaft ; but on the contrary, they were commanded to treat them with every mark of refpect.

Ayder commanded this reftraint to be laid upon them, becaufe the complaint was made at the very time when the revolt of the Nayres demanded his prefence on the coaft of Malabar. On his return to Coilmoutour, and the Bramin Narimrao having renewed the widow's

complaint,

complaint, he fent for the French commandant, of whofe integrity and judgment he was well convinced : " You are, doubtlefs," faid he, " acquainted with the fuit urged by the widow Mequinez againft the Jefuits; and, as I wifh the affair to be terminated by an equitable decifion, I have fixed upon you to take cognizance of the fame, and fhall give you every neceffary power to be her judge." The officer anfwered, " That not being a man of the law, he could not pretend to undertake the diftribution of juftice, for fear of erring through ignorance." Ayder replied, " Certainly you, who are yourfelf a Chriftian, muft be better acquainted with the law * of the Chriftians than any judge in my dominions : and fince my intention is, that every one fhall be judged by his own law, you cannot avoid accepting this commiffion ; but I permit you, if it be neceffary, to felect, as affiftants jointly with yourfelf, fuch officers of your nation and religion, as you think capable of feconding your

---

* Ayder, and all the Mahometans, believe that Jefus Chrift, like Mofes and Mahomet, has given laws to the Chriftians, which the judges are bound to follow in their decifions ; and that Chriftian princes cannot evade them by contrary laws.

own

own endeavours." There was nothing could be objected to this offer. The French officer, after thanking Ayder for the honour of his good opinion, confented to perform his orders to the utmoft of his power : and the day following, Madam Mequinez and the reverend provincial father, being informed of the Nabob's determination, did not fail to wait on the French officer as their judge.

The lady arrived apparently in the utmoft diftrefs. She lamented, with figns of great affliction, that poverty, to which, fhe affirmed, the perfidy of the Jefuits had reduced her, and againft whom fhe vented numberlefs invectives : her oration was fo fpecious that almoft all the Europeans, efpecially the French, who were chiefly young men, were prejudiced in her favour, and were defirous that the Jefuits fhould be condemned to make reftitution, and be burned, or at leaft hanged.

The provincial father was an Italian of about fixty years of age, of a commanding * and venerable

* The Jefuit miffionaries in India, who refide in the country not fubjected to Europeans, call themfelves Bramin Chriftians : they wear a habit refembling that of the Bramins, having the triple cord and the flippers made without the fkin of animals : they wear their

nerable afpect, though at the fame time affable
and mild. He praifed God for infpiring the
fovereign with the choice of fuch a judge as
his heart had long defired. After this fhort
prayer he entreated the French commandant
(making at the fame time the moft humble
apology to the other gentlemen prefent) that
he would be pleafed to grant him a private audience, that he might be able to explain the affair in all its particulars ; but which he could
not do in public, becaufe of certain perfons who
were involved in the bufinefs. The French
officer made a fign for every one to retire ; and
the reverend provincial father, being alone with
him, expreffed himfelf in thefe terms : " You
" muft be fenfible, Sir, that, even in the moft
" regular and holy focieties, it is impoffible to
" prevent Judas' from fometimes appearing ;
" and he who now has drawn this unexpected
" perfecution on us, for the fatisfactory termi-
" nation of which we depend on you, may

beard, and live in the manner of the Bramins, never
eating publicly any thing that has had life, and never
going to the altar without firft wafhing and purifying
themfelves.   Virgins pour veffels of water on their
heads, and afterwards, drying them, they put on the
albe, the chafuble, and other facerdotal habiliments.
This provincial father, like the other miffionaries of his
order, refembled a Bramin.

" juftly

" juftly be called by that name. Before that
" man determined to retire to Goa, there were
" feveral fcandalous ftories came to my know-
" ledge concerning him, that obliged me to
" reprimand him; for, in this country, when
" a man is once at the head of a miffion, the
" fuperior has no other right than that of re-
" primanding him, for fear of a greater dif-
" order. Being informed that my remon-
" ftrances produced no effect, I thought it my
" duty to watch over all his actions. I was
" advifed when he quitted his cure, and that
" he had departed to Mangalor, in his way to
" Goa. I followed him without delay, and
" coming up with him before he embarked, I
" eafily obtained an order from the comman-
" dant of Mangalor to prevent his quitting
" the place before I had publifhed, in all the
" miffions, that if any one had interefts to
" difcufs with that father *, he fhould repair

" to

* All the Chriftian women in India that are married
to Europeans have the madnefs to hoard up a private
fum or fund, which they entruft to their priefts, under
the feal of confeffion. It is to the honour of the miffionaries, that there is no inftance of any complaint of
this truft having been abufed. This cuftom is very
ancient, and feems to have originated with the Portuguefe. The monks, at all events, gain much money

by

" to Mangalor : many perfons repaired thither,
" and among them the dame Mequinez, who
" reclaimed two thoufand rupees, a pair of
" bracelets of rubies, and a collar of pearls,
" which were returned to her ; as was ac-
" knowledged by an authentic act paffed in the
" chancellory of the Portuguefe factory at
" Mangalor, and witneffed by the fignature of
" the French and Portuguefe factors. Since
" the exhibition of the widow Mequinez's
" complaint againft us, I have applied to the
" chief and chancellor of the Portuguefe fac-
" tory * for a copy of the act, which they have
" conftantly refufed.

" To

by the practice, becaufe there are fcarcely any women
that die, who previoufly acquaint their hufbands or relations where they have placed fums in this manner.

* The Portuguefe had a factory at Mangalor, on an
eminence that commanded the river. In this factory
they kept a fmall garrifon of thirty Portuguefe foldiers,
commanded by a lieutenant, who was at the fame time
factor, and a kind of conful : this fettlement had two
pieces of cannon, and difplayed Portuguefe colours.
The kings of Canara fubmitted to this, and the Portuguefe levied a fmall duty, a toll on the entering or going
out of the river of Mangalor, which they pretended to
defend againft invaders. When the Englifh took Mangalor in 1768, the Portuguefe had neither the inclina-
tion nor the power to defend the entrance of the river
againft

" To procure this deed, which is abfolutely
" neceffary for the right decifion of the caufe,
" it will be proper, Sir, for you to make ufe
" of the authority of the Nabob. The bearer
" of his order muft be a Frenchman who can
" be depended on, and who muft compel the
" Portuguefe factor to exhibit the regifters of
" his chancellorfhip, in fpite of all the refift-
" ance he may make, on account of the honour
" of his flag and garrifon. I muft intreat you
" likewife, Sir, to conduct the bufinefs in fuch
" a manner as that the Bramin Narimrao may
" not be apprized of the order given to force
" the chief of the Portuguefe fettlement to com-
" municate his regifters : for I have good rea-
" fons to fufpect that this Bramin, whofe ava-
" rice you are no ftranger to, is interefted in
" the plot, as well as the Portuguefe chancellor
" and factor. The Bramin would not fail, in
" that cafe, to advife them of the intended or-
" der, and they would difpatch the regifters to

againft the Englifh army. Ayder being defirous of
conftructing a citadel at Mangalor, in 1774, M. Catini,
his engineer, found that the fcite of the Portuguefe
factory was the prepereft for building a citadel capable
of defending the entrance of the river ; and the Portuguefe were obliged to refign their factory.

M 3   " Goa.

" Goa. If you cannot clear up the affair by
" means of thefe regifters, you may write to
" Mahé, to know who was the French gen-
" tleman who then refided at Mangalor *.
" You may then apply to him, and perhaps
" his memory will furnifh you with means to
" do juftice to the injured."

The French officer, after having heard the
recital of the provincial father, faid, " Be at
your eafe, my reverend father ; I will do my
utmoft to fearch your affair to the bottom,
without giving any fufpicion of the communication you have made."

Madam Mequinez, impatient to know the
refult of the provincial father's conference with
the French commandant, haftened the next
morning to wait upon him. There were then feveral French officers with him : he no fooner faw
her, than he faid, " Madam, the provincial father made his confeffion to me yefterday ; you
muft now abfolutely make yours." The lady
colonel, affured of the victory, confented with
great readinefs ; and every body having re-

* There was not then, and perhaps never was, a
French factory at Mangalor. The French gentleman,
of whom the reverend father fpoke, was fome merchant
who was cafually there.

tired,

tired, he addreſſed her thus, " How could you thoughtleſsly precipitate yourſelf into the abyſs you are fallen in? You enjoy a great revenue by the bounty of the Nabob; and you have preſumed to impoſe on that prince, whom you know to be ſeyerely juſt : you are a Chriſtian, and you have not ſcrupled to invent the moſt odious impoſture, in hopes of enriching yourſelf by the plunder of the churches and altars, and with the intention of ſharing your unjuſt demands with a Bramin and a Monk, whoſe wickedneſs you are well acquainted with. But it is in vain that you hope any longer to conceal your conſpiracy. I am informed of every thing by the French gentleman who reſided at Mangalor, and who will quickly arrive here, together with the chancellor of the Portugueſe factory, who brings his regiſters, and is guarded by Seapoys. You have but a moment in your power to ſave yourſelf, by making a ſincere declaration of the truth : for from this inſtant I will cauſe you to be arreſted and guarded, without permiſſion to ſpeak to any one; and when your impoſture ſhall be proved, you may expect that the Nabob will puniſh you as you deſerve : but if, on the contrary, you make the con-

feſſion

feffion I demand, I will find means of ter-
minating the affair without noife." The woman, who now faw herfelf unmafked, was
almoft dead at hearing a difcourfe fo unexpected; and finifhed by falling on her knees.
She confeffed the truth, and threw the blame
on the Monk at Goa, and the Bramin, who
had prompted her with this infamous contrivance. The officer raifed her, with the affurance, that by her confeffion fhe had placed
herfelf out of all danger : he then went out, and
faftened the door behind him ; but foon returned with two officers of known difcretion,
to whom he had communicated the particulars
of what had paffed : and the dame Mequinez,
fuppofing them to be of the number of her
judges, repeated before them every thing fhe
had before avowed to the commandant.

The provincial father being fent for, and
informed of the confeffion of the widow, pro-
ftrated himfelf on the earth, and then raifing
himfelf, returned thanks to God, that the
truth was cleared up, and his brethren juftifi-
ed from the accufation fo malicioufly urged
againft them. He neverthelefs intreated the
commandant to conceal the detail of the affair
from the Nabob ; fearing, as he faid, the con-

feguences

fequences that might enfue to the widow ; but more probably wifhing to avoid the enmity of the fecretary Narimrao.

The officer having informed Ayder, that the affair was terminated, that prince was contented with faying, " 1 am perfuaded that the whole is an iniquitous contrivance of the widow Mequinez againft the reverend fathers ; for I am informed, that her conduct is fuch, as, if fhe does not take care, will finifh by bringing no fmall mortification upon herfelf *. However," added he, " fince you and the reverend fathers forgive her, I fhall fay no more

* Ayder propofed to the Swedifh officer, accomplice of Turner the Irifhman, to efpoufe this lady colonel, as a condition upon which he would pardon and reftore him to his former poft. This young man, aged twenty-eight, but of a fpirited difpofition, abfolutely rejected the offer ; faying, he would rather die than marry a woman who had proftituted herfelf to all the Topaffes. His pardon, and permiffion to retire where he pleafed, were the confequence of this anfwer. The lady colonel afterwards married a mongrel Portuguefe ferjeant ; but fhe was highly aftonifhed, when the Bacfi fent for her to let her know that the Nabob had reduced her to ferjeant's pay, becaufe fhe had difhonoured the name of her former hufband, whofe fervices had demanded that the woman who bore his name fhould not be without the means of fubfifting reputably.

of

of it." He immediately gave orders to remove the guard he had placed over the Jefuits. The good fathers were not, however, difpofed to pardon the lady fpiritually : fhe was excommunicated, and condemned to public penance ; to which, though it may feem aftonifhing, fhe fubmitted with much apparent refignation. The provincial father, in his letter, written to inform all the miffians of the means by which his innocence was cleared up, fpoke highly of the French officer ; who, he faid, was in the higheft favour with the Nabob. This eulogium produced a letter from the archbifhop of Cochin, who recommended to him a Malabar prieft, of the number of the Chriftians of St. Thomas, whofe diocefan the archbifhop was. He was deputed, together with three other laymen of his country, to requeft of Ayder the permiffion to keep fire-arms, under the pretence that, by not being armed, they ran the rifk of being robbed by the Nayres and the foldiers of the Nabob. The officer, who imagined he might fafely give credit to the archbifhop's letter, was much furprifed when Ayder faid, he was no ftranger to the antipathy that fomented their quarrel. " Thefe people," faid he, " have been difarmed, becaufe
they

they affaffinated each other, being always at enmity on account of their priefts, who are of different cafts : I fhall take care to place fafeguards in the country, to prevent my people from molefting them, and I fhall fend troops fufficient to difperfe the Nayres."

Thefe Chriftians of St. Thomas are of very ancient origin, being fettled in India before the arrival of the Portuguefe. It is demonftrated, that their St. Thomas was not the difciple of Jefus Chrift. They are partly in fubjection to the Pope, and partly under the patriarch of the Chaldeans, who refides at Merdin in Mefopotamia. This divifion caufes them to deteft each other ; and, profiting by the troubles of their country, they were mutually engaged in a cruel war, when Ayder caufed them to be difarmed. The deputies who came to Coilmoutour were ftout men, with a ferocious air and manner : they had the figure of a fmall crofs above their nofe punctured in the fkin, and a large fcar on the right cheek, caufed by the recoil of their mufquets. The archbifhop, in his letter, offered to the commandant two young flaves, who, he faid, he had himfelf educated, and were qualified to render fervices both of utility and pleafure, being inftructed

structed in writing and in music. As he did not obtain his desire, he sent an inconsiderable present; with an excuse, that the young slaves, at the moment of their departure, had cried and wept so immoderately, that his feelings would not suffer him to part with them. To this present were added a vast number of benedictions, and a promise that he would write to the Pope, then Clement XIII.

The same officer was employed by Ayder in a law-suit between the French and English factors resident at Calicut. A merchant of that city had long been indebted to the French company; and having received a considerable quantity of wood from Ayder, the French factor agreed with him, that he should pay his debt in that commodity, which was much wanted at Pondicherry, or the entire rebuilding that town, lately destroyed by the English. The quantity sold to the French factor being arrived at Calicut, the English factor prevailed on the Raja of Coilmoutour to seize it, on pretence that the English company had a prior claim on the merchant: the Raja, who was gained by the English, adjudged, after hearing the parties, that the English factor should have the wood; which was ac-

cordingly

cordingly carried by him to his factory : but
on the appeal that the French commandant
made to the Nabob himſelf, the Raja ordered
the affair to remain in its then ſtate, till the
deciſion of the ſovereign was known. He
wrote at the ſame time in favour of the Engliſh ; and the French factor, perſuaded of the
goodneſs of his cauſe, begged the commandant of Europeans to intercede in his favour.
This officer having impartially informed Ayder
of the difference between the factors, the Nabob made him this anſwer : " Neither you
nor I are ſufficiently informed to decide on
this affair, eſpecially as our attention is required to things of more conſequence : but, that
juſtice may be done, I have written to the
Raja of Coilmoutour, to put the deciſion
into the hands of the chiefs of the Portugueſe,
Daniſh, and Dutch factors ; and whatever their
judgment may be, to put it in execution."

In purſuance of this order, the delegated
judges decided in favour of the French ; but
the Engliſh factor, to render the judgment il-
luſory, cauſed all the wood to be ſawed up, ſo
that it was rendered unfit for any uſe, except
to be burned : a piece of buſineſs that he could
not have performed without the connivance of
the

the Raja, whofe duty it was to have placed a guard over the wood. The French factor, not being able to receive it in that ftate, wrote to the Nabob, informing him of this difgraceful manœuvre. On the account given by the French officer, Ayder immediately wrote to the Raja to repair to court with the utmoft dif-patch. The governor had no fooner received this order, than, fufpecting the bufinefs, he fent for the Englifh factor and the wood-merchant, and fent the latter to the French factory to of-fer payment of the fum due to the company. The French chief, bound to promote the wel-fare of his employers, could not refufe accept-ing a payment that was much more advanta-geous than the wood; and accordingly gave the merchant a difcharge.

The Raja, furnifhed with this piece, de-parted to wait upon Ayder; who demanded, on feeing him, how the affair was terminated between the French and Englifh? The Raja, without being difconcerted, anfwered with an affected laugh: "The Englifh have loft their caufe; but, as they had fpoiled the wood without waiting for the judgment, I have forced them to pay the value in money; and the French have given the merchant an ac-

I   quittance,

quittance, which he has put into my hands."
Ayder, who was not the dupe of his artifice,
took this occasion to demand an account of the
revenues and disbursements of the country he
governed; and nominated commissioners to receive his accounts. Though the Raja did not
seem abashed at the discourse of his sovereign,
yet he retired extremely chagrined that his stra-
tagem had been turned against himself. On in-
specting his accounts, the committee condemned the governor to pay three or four lacs of rupees * to the Nabob. To obtain either time or
a mitigation of part of the sum, he complained
for some days of the rigour of this judgment;
which he affirmed would ruin him, as he pro-
tested he was not possessed of so large a sum.
On his refusal, Ayder placed guards about his
palace, to prevent water from being brought
him, because, as a Bramin, he was obliged to
wash himself many times in the day. This
step forced him to open a secret repository of
treasure in the very palace in which Ayder

---

* The lac is one hundred thousand rupees. In turning rupees into sterling money, they are, in India,
estimated at thirty pence, or half a crown each, tho'
the average value of the coin does not exceed twenty-
seven pence.

then

then refided, but which is the ordinary refidence of the Raja.

A French furgeon, who had cured him of a
fecret diforder for the fum of one thoufand rupees, half paid in hand, and the other half due,
by a written promife to pay when the cure
was completed, not being able to obtain the
latter five hundred, though the cure had long
been made, thought the prefent inftant favourable to his defire of being paid. Ayder having
heard his complaint, faid, " Do as I did : let
no water come into his houfe till you are
paid." " But I have no foldiers," replied the
furgeon. " But you have friends that have,"
anfwered the Nabob. Upon which advice the
furgeon collected a number of French foldiers,
by promifing them a part of the fum : they
took poffeffion of the palace-gate ; and the wa-
ter-carriers not daring to approach, the furgeon
received payment of his note, to the great diverfion of Ayder, who, notwithftanding what
had paffed, did not remove the Raja from his
government.

Ayder Ali, though in the midft of the moft
brilliant of courts, had become uneafy and
thoughtful fince the departure of Maffous Khan
for Ayder Abad. This lord, after making the

utmoft

utmoſt diſpatch to arrive at the court of Nizam Dowla, Suba of Decan, had diſpatched
letters which removed the ſuſpenſe of Ayder,
and confirmed the intelligence given by the
Iriſh officer. He ſent word that the Engliſh,
by means of the Divan * Rocum Dawla, had
determined Nizam to carry the war into Mayſ-
four ; that all the friends of Ayder had in vain
attempted to diſſuade him from the deſign ; and
that, having given himſelf up entirely to the
ſuggeſtions of his Divan, he had beſtowed the
command of his army on General Smith, who
had brought a conſiderable corps of Europeans
and Seapoys from Madras.

Upon the receipt of this authentic advice,
Ayder determined to defer his expedition a-
gainſt Travancour till a more favourable opportunity, and to march to Syringpatnâm, the
capital of Mayſſour, to be in readineſs to meet
his enemies. Ayder had been long abſent from

* Rocum Dawla was brother-in-law to Mehemet
Ali Khan, whom the Engliſh had made Nabob of Arcot. The title of Divan formerly ſignified the emperor's envoy, charged with the raiſing or receiving of
the taxes and tributes ; but at preſent it ſignifies the
Miniſter and keeper of the great ſeal of the Suba.

this kingdom, in which he firſt ſaw the light, and where his fortune firſt began to diſcloſe it-ſelf. He was about to return, as one of the greateſt ſovereigns in India, to a kingdom he had left in the capacity of a ſubject; for the Dayvas, notwithſtanding their great power, are only the firſt ſubjects of the king. It was the deſire of Ayder to make his entrance with all the pomp and ſtate his rank demanded, and his Savari was therefore very numerous and brilliant. His daily march was a kind of tri-umph.—The deſcription we ſhall proceed to give will be ſo much the more agreeable to the reader, as it will convey an idea of the magni-ficence of the Aſiatic proceſſions.

Ayder left Coilmoutour with a fine army of about fifty thouſand men; of which eigh-teen thouſand were cavalry, extremely well mounted, twenty thouſand Seapoys, and four thouſand Topaſſes, with their uniforms.

Every day of the march the cavalry lined the right ſide of the road by which the Nabob and his attendants were to paſs. The prince was ſaluted by all the officers and the ſtandards. When all the elephants on which the great men were mounted had defiled before one corps

of

of the cavalry, that corps turned about to the left, and rode full fpeed to take their place at the other end of the line. A company of huffars, and one of dragoons, which formed the whole of the European cavalry, took the poft of honour, and were the firft to falute the Nabob ; after which they placed themfelves at the head of the proceffion : they were preceded by fifty couriers, well clothed, and mounted on dromedaries. Next marched two elephants bearing the great ftandards of the Savari, being gold embroidery on a blue ground; one reprefenting the fun, and the other the moon and ftars. After the two elephants marched that which carries the great timbals, called the grand Tomtom : they continually found during the time the Savari is in motion, and may be heard at the diftance of more than a league ; there is even fomething grand and majeftic in the noife ;—the orders of the general are communicated to all the army by means of thefe inftruments. After this elephant came four others, carrying the mufic of the Savari, confifting of fmall timbals, hautbois, flutes, and trumpets, the performers being thirty-two in number. Five elephants, called elephants of war, fucceeded the four :

N 2

they

they carry towers, or a kind of octagon chair, on their backs, which are bound with iron, and strongly fixed to the saddle of the elephant by straps and iron chains. In each of these chairs are six warriors, armed from head to foot in armour which is musquet-proof; their offensive arms being fusils, and a species of blunderbuss of a very large conical bore, that discharge a whole handful of balls at once. One of these elephants is intended for the Nabob, but he never makes use of it in any battle.

The procession of elephants was succeeded by two companies of Caffres or Abyssinian horse. The men were completely armed, one company having their arms polished, and the other bronzed, and both had large plumes of red and black ostrich feathers on their helmets, which hung down their backs to the horses crupper: they bore lances, the steel work of which was highly polished; and the harness of their horses was red, with black silk fringes. The cavalry was followed by a number of men on foot, habited like Caleros; that is to say, almost naked, with large silk scarfs, and close drawers, reaching to the middle of the thigh: they carried long lances,

orna-

ornamented with oftrich feathers and fmall bells, that were made to found by the motion of their march. The Caleros were fucceeded by a body of men carrying fmall banners, or flags of a red ground, with flames of filver.

The lance-bearers ufually follow the prince to the chace : they are habituated to traverfe the mountains and forefts : the bearers of fmall ftandards are fent as fafeguards to towns, villages, and caftles : the appearance of thefe colours is fufficient to prevent the foldiery from entering any place ; but the magiftrates muft attend at the gates or barriers, to furnifh the army, upon payment, with every thing they may want.

After this crowd of people on foot came the *Baras à demi*, or nobility following the court, marching as they pleafed, in order, though without diftinction of rank ; generals, bahaders, and even princes, marched indifcriminately with fimple volunteers. Nothing could be more brilliant than this troop : they were armed from head to foot, and mounted on the moft beautiful horfes : their arms were damafked and encrufted with gold and filver ; many had their cafques orna-

N 3 mented

mented with white feathers, formed of pearls
and precious stones; and great numbers had
coats of mail, gilt and enamelled: the bri-
dles of their horses were enriched with
pearls and other valuable stones, and with
plumes of feathers. The number of this
troop varied every day, they being volunteers; but it was usually about six hundred.
They all had aftagueris *, variously enriched.

The nobility were succeeded by eight ef-
quires or huntsmen of the Nabob, mounted
on superb horses, and followed by twelve
grooms on foot, each leading one of the Nabob's horses, richly harnessed: the first of these
horses was a present from the general of the
Marattas to Ayder, and was extremely singu-
lar: he was of a mouse-grey colour, with a
white mane as brilliant as silver, and so thick
and long, that it reached to the ground; it
was tied together with a ribband; his tail was
answerable in beauty to his mane: but the most
remarkable circumstance was, that he had a
natural covering of a clear bay colour, which

---

* The aftagueri is a parasol, not horizontal but
perpendicular, formed of a rich stuff, embroidered with
gold or silver. It is carried by men on foot at the end
of a long staff, painted and gilt.

I   depended

depended as low as his mid-thigh, and which commencing at the withers, finished at a small distance from the crupper : on this mantle flowers were artificially painted ; so that, tho' the horse was absolutely naked, it was necessary to be very near him, in order to perceive that he was not covered with a cloth of some kind.

After the led horses followed a troop of running footmen, with black staves headed with gold, who were succeeded by twelve ushers or Sauquedars on horseback, carrying silver maces with small crowns at top. After these came the grand officers of the houshold, as the steward, the chief usher, the sword-bearer, &c. they had each a large collar or chain of gold depending on their breast, as marks of their dignity. These officers preceded the grand almoner or Perjada, who marched alone, mounted on an elephant covered with green. He was immediately before the Nabob himself, who rode on the white elephant of the queen of Canara, an animal formerly worshipped as an idol, but now in a state of slavery, having large silver rings on his feet, with chains of the same metal. This elephant, which is said to be equal in value to a thousand others, was far superior to

them

them in height and magnitude: he was covered
with yellow, a colour much affected by the emperor and the Subas. The pavilion in which
the Nabob fat was covered with ftuff of the
fame colour, and had no other ornament than
four fmall globes of filver; except that on each
fide, by filver chains, hung fmall hatchets or
axes, fuch as the Samorin has carried before
him. It is the cuftom of the Indians to affume
the marks of honour of thofe they have van-
quifhed. The elephant bore on his head a kind
of buckler of filver gilt, that reprefented a fun :
he was led by two conductors, the one ranked
as captain of horfe in the Nabob's guard, and
the other was his ufual keeper. In a fmall pavilion behind the Nabob was a valet, to fupply
him with betel; and on each fide an attendant
ftood upright on the foot-ftep, holding by the
pavilion with one hand, and having in the other
a large inftrument to difperfe the flies, made of
white peacocks feathers, which he caufed to
move circularly, and produced a fingular effect
at a diftance. About two hundred elephants followed that of the Nabob, two and two : they
were rode by only three perfons, the mafter,
the conductor, and an attendant in the fmall
pavilion. The coverings and pavilions of
those

thefe elephants were very different in colour and magnificence : fome were bordered with gold and filver lace : many of the pavilions were wrought filver ; and there were fome even enriched with precious ftones, as were thofe of the fon of Ayder, and fome others. The young prince was on the left of his father, and Raza Saeb on his right, but their elephants were not more than half the fize of that of the Nabob.

After all the elephants in proceffion, came what are in India called the honours, borne by five elephants. The firft carried a mofque of gold or filver gilt, and of exquifite workmanfhip, covered with white fattin, that was taken off when the proceffion came near any town or city ; the fecond carried, at the extremity of a red ftaff, the head of a fifh, whofe fcales were formed of jewels and enamel, and a long horfe's tail depended from the fame ; the third carried a large flambeau of white wax in a chandelier of gold, or filver gilt ; the fourth bore two fmall pots of gold, called chambou, at the end of a large red ftaff ; and, laftly, the fifth elephant carried a kind of round chair without a canopy, covered on the outfide with ivory inlaid, and ornamented with gold *. Af-

* All thefe honours are allegorical, and expreffive of the virtues a fovereign ought to poffefs.

ter

ter the honours followed two companies of Abyſſinians on horſeback like the two firſt; and the proceſſion was cloſed by two hundred Caffres on foot, clothed in ſcarlet, with ſilver collars, and armed with lances varniſhed black, and interſperſed with ſilver gilding: all the train was incloſed between a double rank of men on foot, clothed in white ſilk, having lances in their hands about fourteen feet long, varniſhed black, and adorned with plates of ſilver, at the armed ends of which were ſmall red ſtreamers with ſilver flames: the lance-men marched at ſuch a diſtance from each other as to incloſe the whole by joining their lances.

This grand proceſſion, on its march in the plain, had the moſt ſuperb and ſtriking effect.

Ayder was every where received with the moſt lively expreſſions of joy; the higheſt honours were rendered him, and the people crouded to ſee him, while their acclamations, of " Long live Ayder!" were inceſſantly reiterated. Every village, town, and city, was ornamented; triumphal arcs, and other edifices, were erected in various places, according to the riches of the inhabitants; the houſes, and even the walls, of towns and fortreſſes were painted, or at leaſt new white-waſhed; governors, commandants, and other great men, came out in ſtate with

their

their retinues, preceded by muficians, fingers, and dancers, known by the name of Bayaderes, to meet the fovereign ; flowers and fweet water were difperfed in his paffage, and the cannon were heard in all parts of the country. It was in this triumphant march that he met his brother-in-law, Moctum Ali Khan, at the diftance of about a league from Syringpatnam. This potentate was at the head of a numerous retinue mounted on elephants, and marched before Ayder to the ifland, where tents were magnificently dreffed out near the city walls : all the army encamped on the ifland, and the fituation of the camp brought to every one's recollection the great danger Ayder had avoided in the time of Canero at the fame place.

Ayder came into Mayffour without any fear of the events that might arife in the war he fuppofed himfelf to be engaged in with the Suba of Decan : he perfectly knew the indolent and enervated character of that prince, and had no apprehenfions from his army, which was defective in the effential articles of difcipline, arms, and pay, and whofe chiefs, being proprietors of their own troops, were his friends and partifans. From this laft circumftance he was affured that General Smith could make no movements without his receiving advice of them.   As he was abufed by Mirza, his brother-in-law, who every day gave him reafon to think the truce with the Marattas would be foon renewed, he went forward with chearfulnefs, and in fpirits ; and arrived at Syringpatnam with the convic-tion that he could eafily parry every attempt of his enemies.   But his aftonifhment was extreme, when Moctum Ali Khan informed him that there was reafon to fufpect the fide-lity of Mirza Ali Khan ; fince he had learn-ed that the army of the Marattas, to the num-ber of 150,000 men, was on its march from Poni, with the young prince Madurao*, Nana of the Marattas, at their head, who was then beginning his firft campaign ; his march being directed towards Scirra, as Mirza could not but know, fince he had envoys at Madurao's court.

* Madurao was the fon of Balagirao, a Bramin, who had rendered the poft of general of the Marattas here-ditary in his family.   This young prince was then no more than eighteen years old, and poffeffed the moft un-common fhare of virtue and ability : his uncle Raguba caufed him to be affaffinated. Nana fignifies father: it is a name of honour given to Balagirao by the Marattas, which now ferves as a title to his defcendants. The ge-neral being called Nana, the king has no authority, and only acts, like that of Mayffour, in the ceremonies of religion.

5   To

To conceive the trouble and aftonifhment of Ayder at this news, it will be fufficient to know, that Mirza Ali Khan, his brother-in-law and coufin, was the moft beloved by him of all his relations : he had educated him himfelf; and the young lord, endued with the moft eftimable qualities, had always appeared full of gratitude and tender attachment. The great confidence Ayder had repofed in his virtues induced him to think that he could not, in fpite of his youth, place the important government of Scirra in better hands. The only precaution he took was that which he commonly ufed with all his governors, namely, to give him a minifter, or principal fecretary, whofe fidelity he could depend on ; and who had orders to give an accurate account of the conduct of his brother-in-law.

This man, who, like moft courtiers, had concealed his ambition, and the bad principles that actuated him, conceived the hope of making his fortune by means of Mirza. He undertook to gain the confidence of the young prince by flattery, and by condefcending to all his wifhes, or, in other words, to all his weakneffes.

Mirza

Mirza was young, generous, and addicted to pleasure, and diffipated the revenues of his government in his amufements, inftead of referving a part, according to the orders of Ayder. The Bramin, his fecretary, fo far from advifing the Nabob, as he had engaged to do, or at leaft remonftrating to his young mafter, flattered him that he would have time to arrange his accounts, in cafe Ayder fhould demand them, and to amafs a fum fufficient to cover the deficiency, before the Nabob, then engaged in the war on the coaft of Malabar, would think of vifiting Scirra. Mirza fuffered himfelf to be perfuaded by the adulation of his fecretary ; and, continuing his imprudent extravagance, reduced the finances of his government to the utmoft diforder.

Ayder, who thought it proper to keep his brother-in-law in fome fear, and concealed his project of making war on Travancour, wrote to Mirza, giving him commiffion to renew the truce with the Marattas ; and at the fame time acquainted him of his intention to repair to Syringpatnam at the end of the year, and afterwards to Scirra. He likewife gave orders to take, out of the money in referve at

Scirra,

Scirra, a fum fufficient to obtain the renewal of the truce with the Marattas.

This letter, fufficiently perplexing to Mirza in every particular of its contents, gave him much anxiety and trouble: but the Bramin, finding the occafion favourable for averting the ftorm that threatened him ftill more than his mafter, addreffed him thus: "If you have fkill to feize the opportunity that Ayder prefents to you, you will not only be out of all embarraffinent, but may become an independent fovereign. Send me among the Marattas, under the pretence, and with a commiffion to renew the truce, and I will treat with Madurao, and the national council, in fuch a manner, that they will with pleafure acknowledge you fovereign of the country you command; and for a fmall tribute they will engage to defend you, as they defire nothing more than to diminifh the power of Ayder, who has taken this very country from them."

The infinuations of the Bramin, ambition, the pleafure of being independent, the fear of Ayder's arrival, and perhaps, more than any thing elfe, that falfe fhame which prevents young people from recanting an error, determined this prince to betray his truft. He fuffered

fered the Bramin to depart, giving him a commiſſion to treat with the Marattas as he
thought proper. This faithleſs miniſter found
the Marattas very much diſpoſed to liſten to
him. There was an Engliſh envoy at Poni *,
who propoſed to them to attack Ayder, at the
ſame time that Nizam and the Engliſh attacked him on their ſide. The arrival of the
envoy determined the grand national council
to make war on the Nabob ; but Madurao,
though very young, poſſeſſed courage and
greatneſs of ſoul, and would not conſent to
form any alliance with a traitor. " I will
not," ſaid he, " conſent to make war upon
Ayder, unleſs he refuſes to pay the Chotay † ;
and,

* Poni is the ſecond capital of the Maratta country, the reſidence of the general and the national
council, and the place where the army annually aſ-
ſembles.

† The Chotay is the ſeventh part of the revenue of
the Subaſhip of Decan and its dependencies, which
Aurengzebe granted to the Marattas. It is not regu-
larly paid ; but the Marattas raiſe contributions in
conſequence of their claim, which are regulated according to their power, and the riches of the ſtate that
pays them. Ayder, who poſſeſſes conſiderable tracts
of country, as Mayſſour, &c. that owe the Chotay,
in virtue of Aurengzebe's gift, has never ſubmitted to
this

and, in that cafe, the Maratta army will be fufficient to compel him, without requiring an alliance with any one, much lefs with a traitor." In fpite of the generous fentiments of this young prince, it was not in his power to determine the general council; and he was obliged to conform to their decifion.

The very day following that on which Moctum had apprized him of the infidelity of Mirza, Ayder received news of the arrival of the Marattas into the country of Scirra. It was in the higheft degree afflicting to him, when he heard that his brother-in-law, to complete his ingratitude, had joined his enemies with the very army that was intrufted to his charge; and that he had engaged to ad-

this payment; infifting, that no one has any right to compel the people to pay any tax or tribute, except for the good of the ftate, or by the right obtained by fuperior ftrength; that the Marattas being in this laft cafe, he owed them nothing, becaufe God had made him powerful enough to defend his fubjects againft them. He has therefore never made peace with that nation, but only truces for three years, fometimes by paying them a fum of money, and fometimes without paying any thing, according to the fortune of war. It is certain that, in the treaties made between thefe powers, the Chotay is never mentioned.

mit the Marattas into Scirra, and every other
fortrefs in his government.

  An event fo totally unexpected overthrew
all the projects Ayder had formed, and reduced him to the moft difficult plan of defence. For though, upon the falfe advice of
Mirza, he had fuppofed the Marattas were
ready to renew the truce, yet he had concluded that, at all events, he fhould have time
to meet them on the other fide of Scirra ; and,
by joining his army to that of Mirza, he
might give them battle, with Scirra, and the
other ftrong places of that government, behind him, to which he might retire, if neceffary: an event he hoped to fee decided before
Nizam Daulla could arrive with his army on
the frontier of Benguelour, where of neceffity
he muft make his firft attack on him. But
his dominions being laid open by the treafon
of Mirza, he could neither meet the Marattas,
nor the combined armies of the Suba and the
Englifh ; but was forced to wait for them
under the cannon of Syringpatnam, the capital of Mayffour : for the country between that
city and Scirra being a plain, without one
good fortrefs, and his army much inferior to
the Marattas in cavalry, he muft have fought

to

to a great difadvantage, as he muft have run the rifque of a total defeat, without being able to fecure his country from pillage. The numerous Maratta cavalry, habituated to make incurfions, and to fubfift on the ftraw that covers the houfes, would infallibly fpread themfelves over all Mayffour, and might cut off his communication with the magazines of Syringpatnam, and the mountains in its vicinity, which were the only refource to fupport his army; and again, the army of Nizam would probably haften its march, on hearing of the operations of the Marattas: of which concatenation of circumftances, the probable refult would be, that, finding himfelf between two armies, he might be forced to retire into Canara, and abandon Syringpatnam, and the kingdom of Mayffour, to his enemies.

The genius of Ayder, vaft and fertile in refources, feems to have been formed to fhine in critical and embarraffing fituations of this nature. He immediately determined on a plan of action: he divided all his army into fmall parties, and difperfed them over all the country, with orders to all the chiefs to command and oblige all the inhabitants, as well of the country, as of the cities, towns, villages, and

O 2 fortreffes,

fortreffes, to abandon their dwellings, and retire to Syringpatnam, bringing with them all
their property of any kind whatfoever.   The
troops were ordered, at the fame time, to lay
the whole country wafte, without fparing any
thing but the trees ; and to burn all forages,
even to the ftraw that covered the houfes.
To facilitate the devaftation, and the tranfport
of goods, all the futlers, valets, and other
dependants on the army, were permitted to
fhare the univerfal pillage ; and they went
forth on this expedition, attended by every
beaft of burthen belonging to the army or the
city.

It is fcarcely poffible to form an idea of the
promptitude with which this extraordinary order was carried into execution ; and in how
fhort a time one of the fineft and moft beautiful countries in the world was changed into a
defart, for thirty leagues round Syringpatnam.
It is difficult to determine who were the rea-
dieft to fhew their obedience, the inhabitants
or the army : the former abandoned their
houfes, leaving nothing they could carry away,
and they were fucceeded by the troops, one
party after another, who finifhed, by leaving abfolutely nothing. Horfemen and foldiers

were

were continually arriving at Syringpatnam, carrying corn, rice, maize, and even wooden beds and earthen pots, no one chuſing to return empty-handed : and, what may ſeem ſtill more ſurpriſing, all the inhabitants arrived chearful and contented, ſome carrying their children, others their ſick and infirm ; the number of whom, in this happy climate, is always very ſmall. As ſoon as any troop of people arrived, they were paid immediately the value of their effects, at ſo advantageous a price, that no diſpute ever aroſe on the ſubject ; and afterwards they were diſpatched to an allotted part of the neighbouring mountains, where they were allowed a ſufficient quantity of rice and other neceſſaries, at a price much below that which was given for what they ſold at Syringpatnam *.

To

---

* The moderate price of proviſions in the vallies, where theſe inhabitants of the plain went to dwell for a time, ought not to be a matter of wonder, when the abundance at Coilmoutour is reflected on, and it is conſidered, that in the warm climates nothing is required on the earth but water, to inſure good harveſts. The rains are the moſt abundant in the mountainous countries, and the Indians have made vaſt baſons at the feet of the mountains, which preſerve great quantities of water, more than ſufficient for all the purpoſes of agri-

culture.

To remove the furprife, that a whole people chearfully abandoning their habitations muft occafion, we only need obferve, that all the lands are the property of the fovereign, the cultivator being no more than an annual tenant. The Indians of this country, even thofe who dwell in towns, have no other furniture than a bedftead, without covering or tefter, whofe bottom is compofed of withy, and the bed-clothes of the richeft is no more than a carpet; a few chefts of pafteboard to inclofe their linen, fome mats, and utenfils of pottery, without tables or chairs, whofe ufe is unknown to them, as well as three-fourths of the moveables which the Europeans employ; and, as their houfes are built of brick or earth, with very little wood-work, all the damage that the moft mercilefs enemy can do, is quickly repaired.

While the troops were employed in laying the country wafte, the utmoft diligence was ufed in completing the fortifications of the camp, which, on the left, terminated againft

culture. Ayder, inftead of receiving his revenues in money, like the other Indian princes, receives them in provifions; which he difpofes of as well to his own advantage as that of his people.

the

the city ramparts, and on the right at a redoubt fituated at the extremity of the canal,
that, with the river Caveri, forms the ifland
on which the city is built. By this pofition,
the back part of the camp was fecured from
every attack by the canal, which is very broad
and deep, with fteep banks : the front of the
camp was defended by nine large redoubts,
mounting twenty-four, thirty-three, and thirty-
fix pounders, that commanded the whole plain.
About 300 toifes before thefe, on the banks of
the river, were feven other redoubts, flank-
ing thofe before mentioned, each mounting fix
or eight pieces of cannon, and ferved by five
hundred men. All thefe redoubts had ditches
before them, planted with pallifades; and, as
the river was every where fordable, and hard
at bottom, twenty thoufand coltrops were
forged, to be laid as foon as the enemy appeared difpofed to the attack. About one hundred
pieces of cannon from the town ramparts, and
fifty that were in a fortified pagoda fituated on
a very fteep hill on the other fide of the river,
oppofite the part of the ifland fartheft from the
city, would have flanked thofe who might be
difpofed to attack the firft line of redoubts;
and the fame artillery would have rendered

O 4

the

the attack of the second line still more difficult.

In this camp, defended by three hundred
pieces of cannon, it was, that Ayder waited
the approach of his enemies; and, as his cavalry would have been of no use to him, he divided it into two parties; the principal of
which was given to Moctum, who was sent
to meet Nizam in the country of Benguelour, where he made the same devastation as
had been made in the plains near Syringpatnam. As that country is interspersed with
woods and mountains, and contains many
very defensible fortresses, it was not so entirely abandoned : this circumstance furnish-
ed Moctum with better opportunities of har-
rassing the army of Nizam, and carrying off
the foragers, who were of necessity much
spread abroad on account of the waste situation of the country.

The command of the rest of the cavalry,
a small body of infantry, and all the irregular troops, was given to * Mirr Fesoulla
Khan,

* Mirr Fesoulla Khan, is a Mogol nobleman of a
very ancient house. All his family is attached to
Ayder. His brother was Bacsi, or minister of war: he
is a man of a very handsome figure and appearance,
as

Khan, ancient Nabob or prince of Colar, and principal general of Ayder, with orders to repair to the kingdom of Bifnagar, and defend the paffes in the mountains which feparate that kingdom from Canara, and to prevent the Marattas from penetrating, by joining his force to the military eftablifhment of that country. He had inftructions to affift Baffapatnam, the capital of Bifnagar, if the Marattas fhould attack it, and to harrafs the rear of their army, if they fhould advance towards Syringpatnam.

While Ayder was bufied in thefe preparations, to which he was compelled by one of the moft critical fituations it is poffible for a great monarch to find himfelf in, he rode out every day on horfeback, without many attendants, and affected to fhew himfelf often to the army and citizens. His countenance

as fair as an European, very intelligent, of a moft amiable and generous character, but more inclined to expence than his fortune allows: he would be an extremely proper perfon to be fent on an embaffy to Europe. Ayder has a great regard and efteem for him; and his prodigality is one of the qualities that have procured him the confidence of that Nabob, who, like Cefar, is of opinion, *that they who love mirth and pleafure, are not the men who engage in confpiracies.*

was

was not then enlivened with that gaiety that usually diftinguifhes him, becaufe his mind was occupied with the danger that threatened him, and he has not acquired the habit of difguifing his thoughts ; on the contrary, a kind of mild languor or fadnefs appeared in his looks, that would have interefted even his enemies in his misfortunes : his tent was open at all times, and he never was eafier of accefs than at this juncture.

Though every kind of affembly and amufement was forbade, he inftructed his generals concerning the means he thought proper to ufe in his defence, with an air and manner not in the leaft expreffive of embarraffment.

The Europeans of his army, who interefted themfelves with an anxious eagernefs in the fuccefs of the prince, were impatient to know the poft he would affign to them, in cafe of an attack ; for Ayder did not make public his order of battle, and caufed the guards of every poft to be changed daily, though, according to the news, the enemy was on the point of arriving. To fatisfy their impatience, their commandant, with two other officers, waited upon Ayder, and acquainted him that, as he had always conferred upon the Europeans the honour of the
moft

moſt important poſt, they were come to requeſt that he would put the defence of the firſt line of redoubts into their hands *. The prince immediately anſwered, " I had already determined to appoint you to the poſt you requeſt; and the demand you make, on an occaſion when my enemies are innumerable, is ſo much the more agreeable to me, as it is a new mark of your affection : take the command, plant your colours † in the center redoubt ; and you may be aſſured of being powerfully ſeconded, for I myſelf will command the ſecond line, and engage to ſend you the neceſſary ſuccours. I am very much oppreſſed with the treaſon of Mirza, whom I have always treated as my favourite child ; and I have had no reaſon to expect ſo numerous a combination of enemies ; who, ſo far from being provoked, have been loaded by me with benefits : but, notwithſtanding their

---

* The Topaſſes, commanded by European officers, were eſteemed of this number, and the huſſars and dragoons alſo ſerved in defence of the redoubts.

† We have already obſerved, that all the commandant generals have a ſet of colours before their tent ; that of the European commandant was diſtinguiſhed by a cannon with a ball in its chaſe, which denoted his poſt as chief of the artillery, and two ſtreamers above, as marks of his degrees in the cavalry and infantry.

number,

number, I do not defpair. " It is the power
" of God that has raifed me, and I poffefs no-
" thing but thro' him : as long as he fup-
" ports me, I fhall look down on my enemies ;
" and if he fhould forfake me, I muft fubmit
" with refignation to his pleafure."

The fidelity of the commandants of the
fortreffes of Mark Scirra and Maggheri, gave
Ayder all the time his preparations required ;
for thefe officers, when they learned that the
governor general had joined his army to that of
the Marrattas under Madurao, refufed to obey
him: but the general, defirous of poffeffing the
whole country, thought proper to befiege thefe
places, which held out longer than was expected, particularly the fortrefs of Maggheri,
into which a battalion of grenadier Seapoys
had thrown themfelves voluntarily, fimply on the
requifition of the governor of the place, while
they were employed in laying the country
wafte : they made a journey of fourteen leagues
without once ftopping, for fear * of being too
late.

* Their commandant was the fame Cedra Khan
whom the Englifh affirmed they had taken prifoner
near Tillichery : they faid he was brother-in-law to
Ayder, but he is only brother to one of the women of
the feraglio : there is as much difference between him and
a bro-

late. When the fortrefs had capitulated, Madurao was defirous of feeing thofe grenadiers, whofe formation had made fo much noife in India : he was aftonifhed to find thefe brave troops dirty and ill equipped. " I am furprifed," faid he, " that fo powerful a prince as your mafter pays fo little attention to fuch brave men." Their commandant replied, " Defirous of the honour of fighting againft you, we haftened away without any neceffaries but the clothes on our backs ; and we have marched a day and a night without eating or drinking." " I am charmed at your fpirit," returned Madurao, " and fhould be concerned that your mafter, who fent you out well clothed, fhould fee you return in fuch a ftate ; " and immediately ordered them two complete changes of clothes ; adding *, that " tho' the terms of the capitula-

a brother of one of the king's wives, as there is in Europe between a prince of the blood and a relation of the king's miftrefs. All the relations of a fervant (which is the title given to the Nabob's women) are his fervants, and in that quality never fit in his prefence, nor in that of his fons or brothers, whatever may be their military rank ; though all other officers, as low as captains of cavalry, have that indulgence.

* In the Indian capitulations the garifons are never made prifoners of war ; but all the arms, colours, and ammunition, belong to the victors, and the baggage of individuals is fpared.

tion

tion require you to leave your arms and your colours, yet I return your colours as a mark of esteem for your master, and a recompence due to your valour." Thus it was that war was carried on by men we are so ready to think barbarous.

After thus displaying the merit of the Indians, it would be unjust to pass over in silence the spirited action of one hundred European cannoniers of different nations. They had marched, like the others, against the Marattas, supposing they were to fight them; but when they saw Mirza joined his army to theirs, they perceived the perfidy of the governor; and, repairing to their general, "Do you imagine," said one of their officers, "that we will fight against Ayder, whose pay we have so long received? No, our intention is to fight for him, and not against him. Adieu." At the same time they departed, leaving all their baggage, having no other arms but their sabres, because the cannoniers in Ayder's army do no other service than that of the artillery. They arrived at Ayder's camp, without having found any opposition; for Mirza, no doubt ashamed of his treason, gave orders not to oppose their departure. Ayder received them with great pleasure,

and

and gave the officers bracelets of gold, called manilles, and money to the foldiers, paying them likewife the value of their baggage, upon their own eftimation : this daring act of fidelity was perhaps the effect of the difgrace inflicted on the Europeans who adhered to Canero.

General Smith and Rocum Dawla were foon advifed of the junction of Mirza with the Marattas, and announced it to Nizam as a certain prefage of the ruin of Ayder. This news fruftrated all the efforts and intrigues of Ayder's friends in the court of that Suba ; and perhaps thofe very friends, convinced that his ruin was inevitable, might grow cool to his interefts. The Suba being always in want of money to fupport his expenfive pleafures, General Smith found it not difficult to perfuade him to haften his march, without flopping to make any fiege, left the Marattas fhould take Syringpatnam, and feize the greateft part of the fpoils. This forced march, and the time confumed by Madurao in his two fieges, were the caufes that both armies arrived together near Cenapatnam, about feven leagues from Syringpatnam.

The abfolute folitude and defart face of the country, which the enemies perceived in their
approach

approach to the capital of Mayſſour ; the daily loſs of their foraging parties, attacked by different bodies of Ayder's horſe ; and the impoſſibility of obtaining any advice concerning the ſituation and force of Ayder's army, gave the different chiefs of the armies to underſtand that the brilliant hopes they had indulged, of ſharing the dominions and treaſures of Ayder, were not likely to be realized.

As ſoon as the two armies were joined, different corps of horſe appeared in the plain of Syringpatnam. Many advanced ſo near as to reconnoitre the town, and the redoubts in which Ayders colours were diſplayed : as they met with no interruption from Ayder, they rode about the plain, and viewed every thing at their eaſe. The ſame ceremony was performed the following day ; but on the third, at nine in the morning, the plain was covered with the cavalry of both armies, with the chiefs at their head on their elephants : this cavalry was followed by a body of infantry, who brought forward about fifty large cannon, that arrived about noon. The view was grand and ſtriking : the number of horſes was above one hundred thouſand ; and there were more than two hundred elephants.

General

General Smith, at the head of a large body of cavalry, among whom were diftinguifhed various chiefs, though neither Nizam nor Madurao were feen, advanced to reconnoitre the camp. When this cavalry appeared difpofed to advance no farther, a fignal was given from the redoubt in which Ayder was, and the fire poured at once from all the redoubts, from the fortrefs at the head of the bridge *, and from the mountain: this laft did no great mifchief, but terrified Nizam and his army, and convinced General Smith that the projeċt of attacking Ayder in his camp was impraċticable, efpecially for an army whofe chief ftrength lay in cavalry. Towards the evening they who commanded this vaft multitude of men, retired, together with their foldiers, in much diforder, to their refpeċtive camps.

The following day, a council was held with Nizam, at which the chiefs of both armies

---

* This fortrefs is fituated in a bend of the river. It is a good Indian fortification, to which Ayder has added a glacis and covered way, planted with pallifades. The chief difficulty of the attack arifes from the figure of the place, which, forming a crefcent, would enfilade the trench of the enemy.

VOL. I.   P   affifted.

affifted. Every one being defirous of putting his own opinion in practice, no determination was fettled on, though General Smith gave the only good advice; which was, to feparate the two armies, and make feints to draw Ayder out of his camp; but, notwithftanding the propriety of this idea, every one was dif-fatisfied with it, becaufe it fhewed too plain-ly, that their elevated expectations were ill-founded, and required great abatements to re-duce them to probability.

The Maratta chiefs having returned to their camp, no more councils were held; but the two camps remained in the fame fituation, many meffengers paffing between them. The Marattas traverfed the country, as well as dif-ferent corps of Nizam's army: they frequent-ly met the cavalry of Ayder, which almoft al-ways had the advantage; Moctum, efpecially, who is an excellent officer, had the moft de-cided fuccefs. Forages every day became more fcarce, and the capture of the foragers, of horfes, elephants, camels, and oxen, con-tinued to fuch a degree, that they at laft could not be fold at Benguelour at any rate. At length the provifions of rice brought by the merchants were exhaufted, and the price

of

of this indifpenfable article, as well as of every other neceffary, increafed every day. Ayder, who was informed of every thing as it happened, remained at his eafe in his camp, where every thing was in fuch great abundance, that fubfiftence coft fcarcely any thing. The inhabitants, fuppofing every thing would fetch a great price, had laid in vaft ftores; every foldier had a hole in the earth near his tent, filled with rice; the river afforded fifh in abundance; and every kind of country provifions came from the mountains and vallies in the night, attended by a numerous efcort of infantry, after four hours travel through a road interfected by hedges and ditches, where the cavalry would have had no opportunity of fhining.

The Marattas, under the pretence of being nearer to the forages, withdrew from Cenapatnam, and encamped on the Caveri, at five leagues from Syringpatnam. It appears, that they muft have conferred with Ayder previous to the movement; for two days after the change of their camp the truce was concluded on; and on receiving fix lacks of rupees in hand, and fix payable in fix months, they engaged to retire out of his country, and to

reftore

restore Scirra : but the rest of the district in-trusted to Mirza was abandoned to them, and they suffered that governor to remain in pof-session of it, on the condition of paying a small tribute ; for the security of which they retained the fortress of Maggheri : the money was no sooner counted, than the Marattas raised their camp, and departed, taking the road to Scirra.

This news gave the alarm in the camp of Nizam, and that sovereign, more alarmed than the rest, was exceedingly embarraffed. Ayder, who knew his character, and judged it a proper occasion to imprefs him with still more terror, recalled his army from the kingdom of Bifnagar, marched his troops out of the ifland, and encamped in the plain on the road to Cenapatnam.   This manœuvre produced its whole effect on the timid and enervated prince, and difpofed him to liften to the fuggeftions of Bazaletzing, his brother, Maffous Khan, and other friends of Ayder : and there is no doubt, but he would have pro-ceeded in direct oppofition to his Divan, if that minifter, feeing the impoffibility of encou-raging his mafter, had not been the firft to give him the direct advice to treat with Ayder ; and
offered

offered to undertake the negociation himfelf, as
a bufinefs that he was confident might be concluded with the greateſt facility.   To remove
General Smith, and the greateſt part of the
Engliſh forces, he informed that commander,
that fince, in the prefent fituation of things,
provifions and fuccours could only be had from
the country of Arcot, it was neceſſary that the
Engliſh ſhould get poſſeſſion of certain places
belonging to Ayder, to fecure a free paſſage for
the convoys that might be fent from Madras and
the other places dependent on the Engliſh and
Mehemet Ali.

The Engliſh general had not been blind to
the difpofition that prevailed of treating with
Ayder ; but he was happy at an opportunity of
approaching his frontiers, to place himfelf out of
the reach of the perfidy it was probable he might
experience ; and to remove himfelf from a country in which he might be ſhut up, and obliged
to furrender, with all his army, if Nizam chofe
to deliver him up to Ayder.   He wrote an account to Madras of what had paſſed ; and at
the fame time expreſſed his fufpicions of Nizam
and his miniſter : he propofed to make the beſt
treaty they could with Ayder, for fear the
Engliſh ſhould find themfelves charged fingly

with

with a war fo much the more burthenfome as it would be in their own country; and, after having taken leave of Nizam, who loaded him with careffes, from the fatisfaction he had of feeing him depart, he fet off, leaving, however, to the faith of Nizam, two hundred Europeans, one thoufand Seapoys, and fome pieces of cannon.

While the government of Madras received the difpatches of General Smith, Mehemet Ali Khan, Nabob of Arcot, received others from Rocum Daulla, his brother-in-law, which gave him the moft pofitive affurances that Nizam would continue the war againft Ayder, till he had forced him to yield at leaft all the country of Benguelour, and all Malleam, or the Carnatic; that is to fay, the vallies of Coilmoutour, Ceylou, Kifna-gari, &c. : and while he magnified the forces of the Suba beyond the truth, he diminifhed thofe of Ayder; who, he faid, were incapable of prefenting themfelves before the army of his invincible fovereign. The council of Ma-dras, perfuaded by Mehemet Ali Khan, paid no regard to the advice of General Smith, but ordered him to attack the places of Ayder, and to agree with Nizam in every thing; promifing

mifing · to fupply him amply with provifions, ammunition, money, and even troops, if neceffary. At the fame time that this unprincipled Divan wrote thus to Mehemet Ali, he difpatched his other brother, Maffous Khan, to Ayder, to offer to meet him at Syringpatnam, and to affure him, that he was difpofed to do every thing that might be agreeable to him, as Maffous Khan would explain to him. Ayder, on receipt of Rocum Daulla's letter, in order to give fome confidence to Nizam, caufed his army to return to its ancient camp; and wrote to the Divan, that he would be received as became a perfon of his rank and character : it was likewife permitted to the merchants of his camp, and the country people, to carry provifions to the army of Nizam. When this Suba had read the letter of Ayder, he ordered a ceffation of arms, which was likewife ordered on the fide of Ayder; and the Divan fet out with a grand retinue. Ayder met him about a league from Syringpatnam; and, after a fhort converfation, returned to his camp, and Rocum Daulla, having feen the whole Savari of Ayder defile before him, encamped on the fpot. The day following, the Divan came to have audience of Ayder in great ceremony; and,

to lofe lefs time in going and coming, he came
and encamped between the two lines of redoubts: both parties being defirous of concluding, the treaty was made in a few days.
It was agreed, that Tipou Saeb, the fon of
Ayder, fhould marry the daughter of Maffous
Khan, who, as eldeft fon of Anaverdi Khan,
was the lawful Nabob of Arcot: that Maffous
Khan fhould give up all his right to his future
fon-in-law; who, in a few days after figning
of the treaty, fhould be invefted in the nabobfhip of Arcot by Nizam, of whofe fubafhip it is a part: that the two Subas fhould
join their forces to reduce Mehemet Ali Khan,
and thofe who took his part : that, during the
time the two armies acted in conjunction,
Ayder fhould pay fix lacks of rupees per
month, and fhould have the fole right of putting garrifons in the feveral fortreffes of the nabobfhip of Arcot; the command of which
fhould be given to Moctum Ali Khan, brother-in-law of Ayder, who fhould govern the
country in the names of his nephew, Tipou
Saeb, and Maffous Khan : that the former
fhould enjoy the whole revenue of that nabobfhip ; for which Moctum fhould account, after deducting the charge of fup-
porting

porting the troops, and adminiſtering the government.

To unite all the claims in the perſon of
Tipou Saeb, Raza Ali Khan, ſon of Chanda
Saeb, likewiſe yielded up to the young prince
all his pretenſions as well to the nabobſhip
of Arcot, as to Trichnapoli and Madura; and
Ayder and Tipou Saeb, on their part, engaged to give him all the country of Tanjaor,
after depoſing the Raja, as a puniſhment for the
murder of Chanda Saeb, father of Raza : the
country of Tanjaor was underſtood as intended
to be held by him under the ſame vaſſallage
to the Nabob of Arcot as it had theretofore
been held by the former Rajas : and, finally,
the two Subas engaged not to ſeparate, but to
exert all their forces to carry this treaty into
effect.

Previous to the ratification of the treaty
which Maffous Khan undertook to prepare,
the retinue of Tipou Saeb was got ready;
it was compoſed of ſix thouſand of the beſt infantry, of which three thouſand were grenadier Seapoys or Topaſſes, and four thouſand
choſen cavalry, with about three hundred Europeans, including the company of huſſars;
and he likewiſe had the greateſt part of his
father's

father's Savari. Maffous Khan having brought the ratification, Rocum Daulla departed, loaded with prefents, and Maffous Khan accompanied him, in order to affift at the ceremony of the inveftiture.

It will hardly be credited, that Ayder, at the moment of parting with his fon, was in the greateft perplexity and concern, and expreffed it to his friends : " I am afraid," faid he, " of the perfidious and cruel Nizam : he has affaffinated his own brother, will he fpare my fon ? or, at leaft, have I not reafon to conclude that he will detain him, and compel me, by the apprehenfion of my fon's danger, either to pay him a large fum, or to make great conceffions to him ? For, in fhort, I truft my fon in the hands of a wretch to whom nothing is facred." This difcourfe, and many other actions of his, prove that one of the greateft weakneffes of Ayder is his extreme affection for his children and all his relations. However, on the affurances made by Raza Saeb and Mirr Fefoulla Khan (who were charged to accompany his fon, and who protefted they would themfelves perifh before the leaft accident fhould happen to the young prince) he fuffered him to depart, being likewife

wife much encouraged by reflecting on the bravery of the troops and the nobility that attended him.

This little army arrived by a fingle march at Cenapatnam. The whole army of Nizam, and especially the English, officers as well as foldiers, were extremely furprised at their appearance. Though they had heard of Ayder's army, yet they could not conceive how Indian troops, who have always been ill-difciplined, could march in fuch good order, and perform their evolutions with fuch rapidity and exactness. The beauty of their arms and clothing was equally uncommon and ftrange to them; and they were aftonifhed at the pomp of the Savari. The troops were no fooner encamped than the officers came to vifit thofe of Ayder, and continually fpoke with admiration of the excellence of the troops.

The following day Tipou Saeb received a vifit from Bazaletzing, brother of Nizam: he was accompanied by Rocum Daulla, and the principal lords of the court. The fucceeding day the fon of Ayder repaired with all his retinue to the tent of the Suba, who rendered him the higheft honours, and gave him the inveftiture of the nabobfhip of Arcot, with

all

all its dependencies, in the prefence of Maffous Khan and Raza Saeb, the only legitimate pretenders to that territory, and who, by
their voluntary ceffion, left no doubt concerning the rights of the fon of Ayder Ali Khan.
Immediately after this ceremony Nizam difmiffed the few remaining Englifh troops, ac-
quainting them that the alliance he had contracted with Ayder Ali Khan having terminated their differences, he had no farther occafion for their fervices; and that he fhould
write to the governor and council of Madras,
to which place they might retire.

As foon as Ayder was informed that his fon
was acknowledged Nabob of Arcot, he wrote
to his Ouaquil, Menagi Bandec, refident at
Madras, tranfmitting to him a memorial to be
prefented to the governor. The fubftance of
the memorial was, that Nizam Daulla and
Ayder Ali Khan, being well informed that
Mehemet Ali Khan *, by his continual ufur-
pations and intrigues, was the author of all
the troubles that had fo long agitated In-

---

* Ayder was not ignorant that Mehemet was no
more than the agent of the Englifh; but he acted in
this manner to retort their own politics upon themfelves.

doftan,

doſtan, had reſolved to make war upon him,
till they had deprived him of all the territory he poſſeſſed to the excluſion of the proper
and legitimate heirs : that in conſequence they
thought proper to warn the Engliſh againſt
affording him any aſſiſtance ; and required them
to withdraw their troops out of any garriſons
they might poſſeſs in the Nabobſhip of Arcot, or any of the countries uſurped by Mehemet : that neverthelefs, as it was known
that theſe places were pledges for ſums due
to them from Mehemet Ali, Ayder Ali offered to reimburſe them in any ſums lawfully
due, among which he could not reckon thoſe
ſums that were diſpenſed for the purpoſes of
diſpoſſeſſing the Nabobs of Veilour, Vandevachi, and other rightful proprietors, of their
territories ; but, on the contrary, he expected
that theſe laſt ſhould be indemnified from all
the loſſes they had ſuſtained.

It may be eaſily conceived that a memorial
or manifeſto, totally new and uncommon in India, and declaratory of a war againſt the Engliſh, of which they were to bear the whole expence, muſt have cauſed the utmoſt aſtoniſhment to that people. This declaration was
directed againſt the poſſeſſions of the Engliſh,
Mehemet

Mehemet Ali Khan being a Nabob merely nominal, without troops or money, and the flave of the Englifh.

It was the policy of the Englifh in India to traverfe the defigns of the fmalleft potentate, who might wifh to enlarge his dominions, for fear he might arrive to a capability of making head againft them: their adminiftration had long been alarmed at the rapid conquefts of Ayder, and the fudden elevation of his power. In confequence of Nizam Daulla's having ceded to them four northern provinces, they had engaged to furnifh twelve hundred Europeans, and a corps of Seapoys, to the army of that Suba : General Smith, commander of this body of troops, was ordered to infpire Nizam with jealoufy of the conquefts of Ayder ; and to confer with Rocum Daulla concerning the projected war ; offering the Suba all the Englifh forces, and fixing his attention on the immenfe treafures Ayder had found in the kingdom of Canara and the coaft of Malabar ; treafures which they affirmed could not but fall into his hands, as it was impoffible for Ayder to ftand againft the united forces of the Suba and the Englifh.

The Englifh government did not at that time

time indulge the hope of plundering Ayder entirely, but they expected to stop the course of his conquests, and oblige him to abandon the coast of Malabar, among the inhabitants of which they proposed to excite a revolt. By this means their intention was to compel Ayder to yield, either to them or to Mehemet Ali Khan, all the country dependant on Mayssour that lies beyond the great *Gates*, or mountains; which, according to them, ought to be the natural bounds of his dominions. They proposed to leave him in possession of all the rest of his dominions, in the persuasion that it was of advantage to the security and tranquillity of their possessions, that so warlike and powerful a prince as Ayder should be between them and the Marattas *.

But at all events, whether the hopes of the English respecting the war with Ayder were

---

* That it may not be thought that the author of these Memoirs expresses his own ideas rather than those of the princes, governors, and generals he speaks of, he thinks it proper to observe, that these pretensions are collected from a conference between himself and the governor (Bofchier) of Madras, together with Colonel Call, first in council, and chief engineer; in which they attempted to persuade him, that it was the interest of Ayder to make this cession, in order to insure the protection and assistance of the English.

rational

rational or not, it is certain that when they learned that the Marattas had declared war againft him, and Mirza his brother-in-law had joined them, their expectations were unbounded, and they devoured by anticipation the treafures of Ayder.

The council of Madras, who till then had envied the brilliant fortune of the Calcutta adminiftration in the enjoyment of an immenfe territorial revenue, flattered themfelves in a fhort time to realize their chimerical hopes, and to equal them in fplendour and importance. Their letters to the Court of Directors were filled with brilliant projects, that promifed no lefs than the poffeffion of all the coaft from Cape Rama to Cape Comorin : the Court of Directors were thrown into a kind of delirium by their admiration of the profound policy of their fervants ; and every one being anxious to poffefs a large fhare of the Company's ftock, the price rofe to £. 275 *per Cent.* in the year 1768, tho' it afterwards fell at once to £. 220, on the news of the excurfion of Ayder's cavalry to the gates of Madras ; a fall which, to the prefent time, has been conftantly increafing.

Ayder Ali Khan having by his addrefs deftroyed the formidable alliance on which the

2   Englifh

Englifh company formed fuch pleafing dreams, becaufe they knew fo little of the character and power of their allies, and ftill lefs of the enemy whofe ruin they meditated, it became incumbent on the council of Madras to juftify themfelves : for this purpofe they could find no better pretence than to attribute the defeat of their projects, and the war that threatened them in the country of Arcot, to the intrigues of the French.

The defpotifm exercifed in India by the Englifh, againft other European nations, was fuch, that there was nothing they hefitated to do againft any power, whether native or European : they never pardoned other nations the crime of fulfilling their engagements, of whatever nature they might be, with any fovereign, though they themfelves fold mufquets and cannon to every Indian power ; feven-eighths of Ayder's arms being of Englifh make. Their cruelty towards their prifoners, and the barbarity with which they deftroyed Pondicherry, had reduced the greateft part of the French to mifery. The unhappy fituation they found themfelves in after the eftablifhment of the peace, compelled great numbers of them to feek employment and fubfiftence from Ayder and other

Vol. I.   Q   princes :

princes. When any of thefe unfortunate people
'fell into the hands of the Englifh, a dungeon was
the lighteft punifhment they were to expect.
To accomplifh their purpofes they employed, as
will be fhewn in the courfe of thefe Memoirs,
promifes, menaces, and even forgery, to caufe
them to enter into their fervice.

So far from the French government having
had any concern in this war, declared by Ayder, it is certain that no correfpondence with
refpect to that Nabob's operations ever exifted,
either between him and them, or with any officer of Ayder's army, till after the conclufion of
the treaty between Ayder and Nizam ;—truth
obliges me to make this laft exception.   The
correfpondence began by two letters, one from
Ayder, and the other from Raza Saeb, which
thefe perfonages charged the commandant of
Europeans to forward to the governor of Pondicherry.—Here follows the fubftance of the
letters.

Ayder complained in his letter, that the Englifh, without provocation, and after receiving
many favours, had projected his ruin; and by e-
very fpecies of intrigue had formed a league with
the Suba of Decan, and the Marattas, againft
him : that they had attacked his places, without any other inducement than a defire to rob
others

others of their property ; but that he had diffolv-
ed the league made againſt him, by forming an
alliance with Nizam Daulla, for the purpoſe of
making war againſt the Engliſh and Mehemet
Ali Khan, the promoter of their unjuſt aggreſ-
ſion.

He obſerved, that by having formerly affiſted
the French againſt the ſame enemy, and having
ſaved Pondicherry, he had every reaſon to hope
that the French would return him the ſame
good office in ſo juſt a war : that he was not
ignorant of the peace then (1767) ſubſiſting
between the French and the Engliſh ; but that,
while the orders of the French king were expected, he might ſend concealed ſuccours, for
which Ayder would be very thankful, and pay
any price that might be charged for the ſervice
to be done : that, in ſhort, he referred to the
letter of the French commandant, on whom
he had a perfect reliance, and whoſe propoſals
on Ayder's part might be credited as if ſigned
by himſelf, and to whom he might addreſs
himſelf on any ſubject that required ſecrecy.

Raza Saeb wrote, that his family had always
been attached to the French ſince their firſt
eſtabliſhment in India : that in conſequence of
his inviolable attachment, his father had loſt

Q 2   his

his life, his mother was prifoner at Madras, and he himfelf had loft every thing : that an opportunity now prefented itfelf of repairing his fortune in fome meafure, by the affiftance of his friends : that he hoped to find his moft ancient allies, the French, difpofed to affift him againft thofe who had unjuftly robbed him, and were the caufe of all his misfortunes : he concluded his letter, like Ayder, by referring to the French officer for details, having, as he affirmed, the moft unbounded confidence in him.

These letters were fecretly carried to Pondicherry by the Perfian writer of the commandant, a man deferving the moft abfolute confidence, and who had been long attached to the French nation, having been employed by M. Lally at Pondicherry, where his refidence had been for above thirty years, and where his wife and children then were : the letters were put into the ftock of a piftol, which this man wore at his girdle, walking on foot, and leading an ox loaded with feveral wares of the country, like a petty merchant or pedlar.

To anfwer the truft thefe two princes repofed in him, and to fulfil his duty to his king and country, the commandant difpatched a letter, together with thofe of the Nabobs.

After

After confirming the refolution taken by the two Subas to carry on the war on the coaft of Coromandel, he gave an exact detail of the forces of Ayder, and thofe of Nizam; and, to fhew that he fpoke with a knowledge of the bufinefs, he likewife gave an account of the Englifh forces. He demonftrated that it was impoffible for the Englifh to fecure themfelves from lofs in this war, becaufe their former fucceffes in India arofe from their wars being carried on near the fea-coaft, or on the banks of the Ganges, which gave them a facility of conveying ftores and ammunition by fea, and receiving other affiftance from their veffels; whereas, in their conteft with Ayder, they would be deprived of thofe advantages, the war being to be carried on in a country remote from the fea, without one navigable river; where the fortreffes are fpread at great diftances from each other; and where every advantage would depend upon cavalry, of which the Englifh were entirely deftitute: that the army of Ayder was totally unlike thofe of the other Indian powers, the duty being performed with regularity: and that, if the Englifh placed any dependance on night attacks, furprizes, or treafon on the part of his

Q 3 generals,

generals, they would find themſelves miſtaken : that he himſelf, being intruſted with the ſafety and preſervation of the army, could with the moſt abſolute confidence promiſe to inſure it from any ſurprize ; and that the treaſons ſo frequent in the other Indian armies could not take place in Ayder's, becauſe the generals had no property in their troops, all the officers, horſemen, and ſoldiers, having but one maſter: and, concluding that Ayder would have the advantage, he adviſed that an exact and abſolute neutrality would not be the moſt prudent mode of action, becauſe it would of neceſſity diſpleaſe both parties *. But the medium he adviſed was, to ſend ſome ſmall ſuccours to Ayder, promiſing to ſend more ; the performance of which promiſe might be delayed at pleaſure, by throwing the excuſe on contrary winds, that prevented the arrival of ſhipping. As the force at Pondicherry was but ſmall, no great force could be ſent from thence, but it would be ſufficient to ſend ſome officers

* Ayder and Raza Saeb requeſted ſuccours, as a return for their former ſervices ; and Mehemet Ali Khan demanded that the French ſhould ſupport him, as Nabob of Arcot, acknowledged by the treaty of Fontainebleau.

and

and good gunners, who might join the army as deserters, without embroiling the nation, whose interest it was to see the power of the English in India depressed. The officer added, that as a faithful subject of his king, and from the daring character of Ayder when he is attended with victory, he judged it proper to advise the governor to fortify Pondicherry as early as possible, were it only by clearing the ditches, raising the ramparts with dry earth or the ruins of the old works *, and mounting a few cannon on the bastions; because, if Ayder should approach Pondicherry, and perceive it without defence, he might lay aside the respect due to the French colours, and take all the artillery, and other matters he might be in need of, as payment of his due for the succours formerly granted the French : at the same time the officer assured the governor, that if any violence or want of respect for the king's standard should be shewn, he might depend upon the co-operation of about eight hundred Europeans, who were in Ay-

---

* The new fortifications of Pondicherry were then scarcely began; but the governor, immediately on the receipt of this letter, gave the place an appearance of being in a state of defence.

der's army. The letter was concluded, by advising the governor to purchase rice and provisions for Pondicherry, by taking advantage of the abundance then in the country, and the fear the inhabitants were in of being plundered by the Indian armies ; because the resolution was taken to lay the whole country waste by the cavalry and irregular troops, as was really done afterwards — (the French governor profited by this advice, and was in consequence able, during the whole war, to keep the price of rice at Pondicherry at less than half its value at Madras): and, lastly, the officer added, that to forward the good disposition of Ayder and his allies, it would be proper to send M. B . . . ., or some other person esteemed by Ayder, on an embassy, to compliment the two Subas.

The receipt of these dispatches gave the governor infinite pleasure, as they dispelled his fears concerning Ayder, whom he justly considered as the natural ally of France. But, from experience, having a very low opinion of the bravery of Indian troops when they fight against Europeans, he could not adopt the ideas of the French commandant of Ayder's army : besides which, the Company's instruc-

tions,

tions, then fubfifting, were fo precife in commanding him to avoid every fubject of con-
tention whatfoever, and particularly with the
Englifh, that he thought himfelf obliged to
anfwer thefe letters in a manner very different
from what had been expected.

His letter to Ayder began by felicitations on
the glory he had acquired by his conquefts, and
the glorious peace he had made with his numerous enemies, who were become his allies : he
obferved that it was with concern he heard that
war, which is always ruinous to nations, was
about to commence on the coaft of Coromandel : that he wifhed the Nabob every kind of
profperity, and would not fail to fend an embaffy to compliment him when he came near
Pondicherry ; but that he was exceedingly concerned at its being out of his power to difpofe of any troops againft the Englifh, becaufe
the two nations were at peace, which he could
not infringe without new orders from the king
his mafter, to whom he would write without
delay : and, laftly, he referred to the French
commandant, who had forwarded the Nabobs
letters, and who, he faid, would explain fuch
matters as required detail.

The

The letter to Raza Saeb was to the fame purport. In anfwer to the officer's letter, the governor advifed him, that, by difpatching the letters of the two Nabobs, he had fubjected him to the rifque of breaking with the Eng-lifh ; that he earneftly begged he would fpare him the confequences of fuch a correfpon-dence, as he could not render a greater fer-vice to his country, in the then fituation of the French in India, without troops, and without fortifications : that in the mean time he would not fail to reprefent his compliance to this re-queft in its true light to the minifter, and the Eaft India company ; and he might depend on his informing them of the fervices he had ren-dered them by the important advices contained in his letter : that, from his own unhappy ex-perience of the pufillanimity of the Indians, when they combat with Europeans, he had reafon to fear that the future war would not turn out to the advantage of the two Subas : that he could not, in any manner, afford af-fiftance either to Ayder or Raza Saeb, his orders being too precife in directing to give no fubject of complaint to the Englifh, or to Mehemet Ali Khan : that he begged he would explain thefe reafons to the two princes who

had

had written to him, foftening his refufal as he
judged beft : and, more efpecially, he begged
him to write no more directly to him, but
that he fhould be glad to hear news of his
negociation by a letter in cyphers, which he
might fend by way of M....

There is no room to reproach this governor
for his faithful and ftrict obedience to his orders. It is to be wifhed they had been lefs
precife, as he might then have profited by this
opportunity, that the miniftry could not pof-
fibly forefee ; by a correfpondence with Ayder, he might have animated him to a war a-
gainft the Englifh, that would have been ruinous to their Company ; and, by anfwering the
wifhes of that prince in a very flight degree,
might have prevented certain events that im-
peded his progrefs, and which obliged him to
make peace, and referve himfelf for another
opportunity of enforcing his fon's juft pretenfions to the Nabobfhip of Arcot.

This governor gave advice to the minifter
and the Company of the approaching invafion
of the coaft of Coromandel by the combined
armies of the two Subas : and at the fame
time he communicated his fears for the event

of

of the war, which he confidered as neceffarily productive of the ruin of Ayder; who would, he faid, have been a very ufeful ally, if the French officer (commandant of Europeans) wanting experience, had not carried him to this extremity, but had referved him for the time of war between England and France;—an expreffion dictated by the European prejudice, which leads us to imagine that the inhabitants of the other parts of the world have not received from nature the fame portion of reafon and judgment as ourfelves, to determine for themfelves according to their own intereft, rather than to follow the moft fpecious reafoning that can be offered to the contrary. It is to be prefumed that, on the fimple expofition of the facts, or from the copy of the French officer's letter, the miniftry had taken thofe refolutions, upon receiving the news of the invafion, which were not determined on till the end of 1769;—refolutions that would have been fatal to the Englifh empire in India, if the differences relative to the Falkland Iflands had not been made up.

Ayder, after having determined to make a defcent on the coaft of Coromandel with Ni-

zam

zam Daulla, took every precaution to prevent interruption from other parts : he was fenfible of the importance of the war he was engaged in, and which was to be tranfacted with enemies fo much the more to be feared, as they knew how to fight. By the advice of his European commandant, he gave up the idea of forming a corps of European infantry, on account of the impoffibility of making them fufficiently numerous to face a fingle Englifh regiment : he therefore determined to incorporate all his European foldiers either among his huffars or dragoons, or among his artillery, except fuch as were made officers of the grenadier Seapoys or Topaffes ; which was the corps of infantry deftined to face the Englifh troops. The artillery of his army was likewife confiderably augmented ; and he took proper meafures to have always an immenfe quantity of ammunition, fuch as it was impoffible for any European army to convey after them, or indeed for any other army that was not perfectly affured of its rear.

The Indian armies have great quantities of baggage, carried by oxen and camels, but chiefly by oxen, the camel being fit for little befides parade : for this animal, on account of

its

its flefhy feet, cannot be fhod, and is incapable of travelling either on a ftony or a muddy clay foil, being apt to fall; it is likewife with difficulty made to pafs a river; and is, befides, abfolutely incapable either of afcending or defcending a mountain when loaded. Befides the baggage of the army, it is followed by a great number of * merchants and workmen of every kind, who have many beafts of burthen.   Ayder gave orders that all thefe, not excepting thofe of the fovereign, fhould carry a ball, from twelve to fix-and-thirty pounds, for which the proprietor of the beaft fhould be anfwerable.

A horde, confifting of a kind of Bohemians,

---

* Thefe merchants are the purveyors of the army, and render it unneceffary for the fovereign to provide other commiffaries : it is fufficient for the general to keep the paffages free, and to inftruct them, by the Cotual or provoft, of the quantity of rice in the army. Rice, which is the only grain made ufe of either by the Indian or European troops, does not require to be made into bread ; and confequently there is no trouble of conftructing ovens, which would be neceffary in furnifhing an army with bread: however, the officers, and all who chufe to go to the price, may have excellent bread in the Indian armies, which is baked in portable ovens, a kind of utenfil that might be introduced with great advantage into European armies.

very

very numerous in India, of unknown origin, inhabitants of the woods (whom the prejudices of India has forbidden to dwell in walled towns, becaufe it is faid they eat every kind of animal or reptile) was permitted by Ayder, who is above prejudice, to follow the army, and fell milk, wood, and every thing their induftry could procure. Thefe men undertook to convey a confiderable part of the powder, by means of their little carriages, drawn by buffaloes: to affift them in procuring a fubfiftence, part of them were taken into pay as pioneers, and were of the greateft utility in fieges and the conftruction of intrenchments, or repairing of roads, as well by carrying earth as by making gabions and fafcines.

The harnefs of all the cannon and artillery was doubled; and, that nothing might retard their march; every piece of eighteen pounds or upwards was provided with an elephant *.

The

* It can hardly be imagined how ufeful thefe elephants are, nor with what fkill and intelligence they do their work. When a piece of artillery is drawn up a hill, the elephant is behind it, and fuftains it with his foot, while the oxen paufe to take breath: if the piece is going down a hill, the elephant retains it by a rope faftened to his trunk: if the tackle gets entangled, or if the piece overfets, or fticks faft, he affifts the

The ammunition waggons carried two hundred charges of powder, and an immenſe number of cartridges, for the muſquetry. Every battalion of grenadier Seapoys had two four-pounders in its ſuite.

While theſe different preparations were making, Ayder arranged every affair relative to his dominions, ſo as to be out of apprehenſion of any unexpected event happening in his abſence.

The truce with the Marattas, and his alliance with Nizam, delivered him from the fear of any foreign enemy, and permitted him to employ his whole force againſt them, by depriving them of the means to create diſturbances by their intrigues. He reſtored their dominions to the different Nayre princes, on condition of an annual tribute, which he propoſed to demand, or to let accumulate, according to the

---

the oxen according to the circumſtances. An officer of reputation, then major of artillery, but now (1782) reſident at Paris, affirms, that he has ſeen the elephant of a piece of cannon (out of patience to ſee that the oxen did not draw, in ſpite of the whips of their drivers) cut a branch off a tree, and beat thoſe animals till they acted as he thought proper.—When the piece is brought before the battery, the elephant himſelf places it in the embraſure, without any aſſiſtance.

fituation of his affairs; and withdrew all his troops from the coaft of Malabar.

The French commandant at Mahé, and the Dutch at Cochin, employed themfelves with effect, to terminate the difference between Ayder and the Nayre princes; and to their efforts it is that the coaft of Malabar is indebted for peace.

An important difcovery, totally unexpected by Ayder, and which was made foon after the conclufion of the truce with the Marattas, occafioned an event that has induced many perfons in India to fpeak againft Ayder.

It was difcovered, that Nand Raja, ancient regent of Mayffour, whom Ayder called his father, had joined with the Marattas and the Englifh in the general confpiracy againft him. Nand Raja then refided at Mayffour, a fortrefs two leagues diftant from Syringpatnam, the capital of the lands he held *en appanage.* Ayder was exceedingly embarraffed, when he difcovered this treachery: the great age of the prince made it improper to propofe his marching againft the Englifh: to leave him in his refidence, and to give the government of the kingdom of Mayffour to another, would have excited his complaints, and might have fur-

nifhed

nifhed him with an occafion to excite new
troubles.

The pretence made ufe of by thofe who irritated Nand Raja againft Ayder was, that this
laft, after having conquered the kingdom of
Canara, and fixed his refidence at Nagar, ought
not to have given the regency of Mayffour to
any one but Nand Raja : but, without confi-
dering the advanced age and incapacity of
Nand Raja, which alone would have prevented
him from taking that ftep, he was reftrained by
his promife to the old dowager Dayva, who
had always been the mortal enemy of her brother-in-law, and was apprehenfive of being
fubjected to his power. Ayder, in gratitude for
the fervices rendered him by that lady, could
not confent to difpleafe her in this refpect ; but
as fhe was the object of the pleafantry of all the
court, on account of the irregularity of her
manners, it was whifpered that Ayder made
the old lady believe that Nand Raja demanded
the government for the purpofe of punifhing
her for the little refpect fhe bore to the laws,
and the manes of her deceafed hufband ; by
which means he obtained large fums of her,
either in the way of gift or loan ; giving her
likewife to underftand, that he was diftreffed

fed for money to pay for the Maratta truce, and his alliance with Nizam ; and it is likewife probable that he did not forget to fay, that Nand Raja offered large fums for the appointment of regent. Thus it was that Ayder, from motives of intereft rather than policy, took a pleafure in fomenting the difcord between the brother and fifter-in-law. An opportunity prefented itfelf of doing this on the occafion of the death of the king of Mayffour. Nand Raja wrote to folicit the title of king for the younger fon, in preference to the elder, who he affirmed was weak, and incapable of the office : but his letter availed little with Ayder, who was folicited by the widow Dayva in favour of the elder : he wrote, in anfwer to both, that not being able at that time to attend any thing but the war with the revolted Nayres, he had given orders to Moctum Ali Khan, to place on the throne that prince, of the late king's fons, whom he might think the moft worthy to reign : he wrote fecretly, by the fame courier, to Moctum, to place the youngeft on the throne. This proceeding, which, as may be readily imagined, excited the complaints of the widow Dayva, and of moft part of the nobility of the kingdom, gave Ayder an opportunity, on his arrival at

R 2 Syringpatnam,

Syringpatnam, to make a parade of his equity, by giving the throne to the eldeſt. The whole buſineſs drew an additional ſum from the old lady, and created many enemies to Nand Raja, and perhaps to Moƈtum, who readily aſſiſted in all theſe artifices, through his unbounded attachment to his brother-in-law.

It not being praƈticable either to give Nand Raja the government of the kingdom, nor to remove him out of it, and ſtill leſs prudent to leave him diſcontented in the abſence of Ayder, a council was held on the buſineſs ; the general advice was to ſecure his perſon, at leaſt during the abſence of the Nabob, and in the mean time to remove from him a Bramin, his brother-in-law, who gave him bad advice : but to this Ayder oppoſed the written promiſe he had made to the Raja, *never to make any attempt on his liberty, property, or life,* beſides the difficulty of arreſting that prince in his reſidence at Mayſſour, a place capable of ſtanding a ſiege, and where Nand Raja had upwards of two thouſand troops, forming, it muſt be confeſſed, the whole of his little army.

This affair being of ſuch a nature as to require a ſpeedy determination, it was agreed, that Ayder ſhould go the following morning in
grand

grand ceremony to Mayſſour, to make an honourable viſit to Nand Raja, and invite him to
come and encamp with his little army in the
iſland of Syringpatnam, in order to make his
public entry into the capital in quality of viceroy, as Ayder was deſirous of inveſting him with
that dignity before his departure : the viſit
was accordingly made, and Nand Raja, at the
height of his wiſhes, arrived with his family
in the iſland, under the power of Ayder; who
that very day, under pretence of exerciſing his
troops in their evolutions, inveſted the little
camp, and incloſed it in the night by detachments of infantry, who were ordered to ſuffer
no one to paſs them, without firſt conducting
him to the Nabob, to be queſtioned by him.
As it had been difficult to perſuade Ayder to
ſecure the old man, it was eaſy for Nand Raja
to perceive that he was under guard, which put
him into ſuch a rage againſt the Nabob, that he
carried his views to an exceſs that might have
been fatal to any other prince but Ayder.

The unfortunate Raja ſent a meſſenger to
the Perſian writer, named Mirr Saeb, ſecretary
to the French officer, and who had been charged with the letters to the governor of Pondicherry : his pretence was to enquire whether

R 3   he

he could not procure from Pondicherry fome crude falt of tartar and other European drugs; the Raja being a chemift, or rather alchemift, who had worked many years to difcover the tranfmutation of metals. The Perfian being alone with Nand Raja and the Bramin, the former propofed to him to acquaint his mafter, that if he would affaffinate Ayder, he (Nand Raja) would depofit the value of eight lacs of rupees in gold, filver, precious ftones, and clephants; the irritated old man being determined to ftrip himfelf of all his property rather than not fatisfy his vengeance againft his fuppofed enemy: the project, he obferved, was eafy to be put in execution, becaufe the Nabob, on his return from the excurfion he made every two days, paffed the night by the light of flambeaux before the camp of the Europeans; and nothing could prevent their feizing this inftant, and fhooting him by an aim taken from the infide of one of the tents. The writer, according to his own account, not daring to fhew the horror this propofition made in his mind, promifed to fpeak on the fubject to his mafter, and to give an anfwer the following day to a Bramin who was fhewn to him; and who promifed to wait at the gate of

a fmall

a fmall pagoda indicated to him. The writer made hafte to inform his mafter of the interview he had had with the Raja, and the abominable commiffion he was charged with: the officer, after recovering from the indignation this bafe propofition naturally produced, ordered him to keep the whole a profound fecret*. Fortunately this officer had been one of the council, in which the affair of Nand Raja had been difcuffed ; he knew, confequently, that on that very day the Nabob was to decide whether Nand Raja fhould be arrefted, and to direct in what manner it fhould be done. The ftorm that was ready to burft on the head of Ayder did not permit the commandant to defer any longer the waiting upon him ; he therefore went, with a determination either to conceal or relate what had come to his knowledge, according to the difpofition he might find Ayder in, with regard to arrefting Nand Raja : when he came into the

---

* The writer was not exact in his obedience, for he communicated the whole to Mirza Ali Naki, who had been commandant of Seapoys at Pondicherry under Meffrs. Lally and Leyrit, a man of great merit, efteemed by Ayder, and much attached to the French : he did not fail to acquaint the French officer of the indifcretion of his fecretary.

R 4   prefence

prefence of the Nabob, that prince addreffed
him in private : " That old fool, Nand Raja,"
faid he, " has fent for your Perfian fecretary to give him a commiffion to procure
drugs from Pondicherry ; Has the man mentioned it to you ?" " Certainly," replied
the French officer, " he has given me an account of his interview, and I cannot but advife you, after what I have heard, not to
delay a moment in arrefting Nand Raja."
" It is a decided ftep," returned Ayder, " every
thing is arranged for that purpofe ; he is to
make his public entry the day after to-morrow into Syringpatnam, at the head of his
troops. The ftreets he paffes through will be
lined with grenadier Topaffes, or Seapoys, and
at the palace there will be placed an entire battalion : his troops will be arranged on the
parade in readinefs to relieve the pofts as they
are quitted by the grenadiers ; Moctum has
undertaken to difarm the troops and all his
people ; and, leaving him only his women and
a few domeftics, will confine him in his own
palace ; and, fince the old man is without abilities, and, no one can rely on him, every thing
will be performed without trouble, before the
cannon of the place falute Moctum, who will
quit

quit his government to-morrow. Send as many Europeans into the town as you can, as cannoniers: let them enter by fmall parties, and through the feveral gates, and unite, as if by curiofity, about the palace of Nand Raja. Do not go yourfelf, but command your officers to obey punctually the orders of Moctum, or his brother Ifmael Saeb."

The little attention paid by Ayder to the manner of the French officer when he infifted on arrefting Nand Raja, fhews how far he is from being inclined to fufpect thofe who have gained his confidence.

This is not the only proof of the opennefs of his character, that Ayder has given the fame officer: for that very night, after returning from the Dorbar *, being gone to reft, he was informed from the prince that the chief ufher and fword-bearer of the Nabob defired to fpeak with him on an affair of the laft importance, which they could communicate to him in bed, without his getting up. Being introduced, they faid, " The guard which, as you know, is placed round the camp

---

* The Dorbar is, properly fpeaking, the council, or place where it is held; but the word is commonly ufed to denote the court.

of Nand Raja, ſtopped one of your people,
a ſhort time ago, coming from thence;
and, though he ſaid he belonged to you, it
was thought proper to conduct him to the Nabob, becauſe his orders on that head are very
preciſe. The man, in paſſing by your guard,
called for help; and the guard, knowing * him,
took him out of the hands of his conductors,
and ſet him free. The Nabob has therefore
ſent us to beg you will ſend the man, that he
may be known by thoſe who arreſted him :
he has alſo charged us to give you his word,
that as ſoon as it is certain that he is one of
your people, he will ſend him back, for you
to do what you think proper with him."

The officer, much aſtoniſhed at this news,
which he ſuppoſed to have ſome relation to the
Perſian writer, ordered enquiry to be made of
the guard, concerning the man they had libe-
rated : to which his valet-de-chambre anſwered, " He is a black Peon †, whom I ſent to

* According to the privileges granted to the Europeans, all deciſions reſpecting juſtice, among them and
their dependents, are made by themſelves.

† A Peon is a black ſervant, who carries a bandalier, with a plate or tablet of the arms of his maſter,
and who runs before his palanquin.

the

the camp of Nand Raja before midnight, to procure fome manna, as I was informed that a druggift of that camp had fome. This Peon, having met an acquaintance, amufed himfelf till after midnight, knowing he was not wanted : on his return he was arrefted, which he fuppofed improper, on account of the protection of your bandalier he carried ; he therefore called out as he paffed your guard, and was fet free." The officer ordered the Peon to be fent for, and put him into the hands of the prince's officers, by whom he was conducted into the prefence. The guards immediately knew him, and Ayder was contented with afking him this queftion, " Did you come from Pondicherry with your mafter ? " And on his replying in the affirmative, he fent him back, and the affair was thus terminated.

On the day appointed, Nand Raja, without any miftruft, made a pompous entrance into Syringpatnam, at the head of his little army, the cannon firing, and the troops beating to arms, and faluting him. Being arrived at his palace, his attention was taken up by the compliments of the great men of the city, who were admitted by few at a time, on the pretended

tended account of not making too great a
crowd. Moctum then entered the city, followed by a number of officers, and made a
fign to the troops, not to pay him any honours : he went directly to the palace of Nand
Raja, where every one fuppofed he was going
to pay his refpects ; and difmounting, he caufed
the firft company of the battalions of Seapoys
who guarded the gate, to follow him. As
foon as he came into the prefence of Nand
Raja, who came to meet him, he acquainted
him, that Ayder, being informed that he was
furrounded by people who gave him bad advice, had fent him to remove them from about
him : at the fame time he commanded all prefent to leave the palace, which was done without uttering a word ; the grenadiers followed
them ; and Moctum remaining with Nand
Raja, his two fons, and fome officers, the
converfation was carried on with the greateft
politenefs. Moctum acquainted the two princes
that they were to make the campaign ; and
that, inftead of one father, they would find
two in Ayder and himfelf. During this fhort
converfation, the women and all the family
of Moctum were announced. Moctum took
his leave, carrying the two princes with him,

to

to whom he reprefented, that it became their
dignity to wait upon the Nabob, and give
him an account of all that had paffed.   Thefe
young noblemen departed, accompanied by
many of Moctum's officers; neither they nor
Nand Raja expreffing the leaft aftonifhment
or chagrin.   After their departure, Moctum
fpoke a word to Nand Raja's general, who
ordered his troop to ground their arms, which
was done with great filence.   All the gates
and windows of Nand Raja's palace, that
looked towards the ftreet, were afterwards
walled up, except the principal entrance;
which is no great disfigurement in an Indian
palace, whofe principal front lies towards the
gardens.   Then it was that Nand Raja, to
the great fatisfaction of the dowager Dayva,
found himfelf fhut up in his own palace.
Ayder paid the arrears due to his troops, which,
for the moft part, enlifted among his own.
On the valuation of the Raja's income, it was
found to be equal to four lacs of rupees: two
of which were allowed him for his own maintenance, and the other two were given to his
fons, who made the campaign with a brilliant
equipage, under the conduct of their father's
old general, who appears to have been in intelligence

telligence with Ayder in the tranſaction juſt related.

All the preparations for the campaign being made, the two armies began their march; that of Nizam took the road of Oſcota, and that of Ayder paſſed by the way of Benguelour.

When they had arrived, and encamped at the gates of this city, ſeveral councils were held, to determine on the operations, and take the neceſſary meaſures: Bazaletzing, Rocum Daulla, and ſeveral other chiefs, aſſiſted at theſe councils. It was agreed, that the two armies ſhould march always ſeparate, but at ſuch a diſtance as to aſſiſt each other in all their operations: that the army of Ayder ſhould take the avant-garde till they had paſſed the mountains: and that, when they had entered the kingdom of Arcot, it ſhould again be conſidered, whether it was beſt to act ſeparately or conjointly.

END OF THE FIRST VOLUME.